AF560092

HANDBOOK OF PETROLOGY

HANDBOOK OF PETROLOGY

By

Dr. Veena

Dept. of Zoology
M.M.H. College
Ghaziabad (U.P.)
(India)

DISCOVERY PUBLISHING HOUSE PVT. LTD.
NEW DELHI-110 002

Published by:

Tilak Wasan

DISCOVERY PUBLISHING HOUSE PVT. LTD.

4383/4A, Ansari Road, Darya Ganj

New Delhi-110 002 (India)

Phone : +91-11-23279245, 43596064-65

Fax : +91-11-23253475

E-mail : parul.wasan@gmail.com
discoverypublishinghouse@gmail.com

web : www.discoverypublishinggroup.com

***First Edition:* 2012**

ISBN: 978-93-5056-096-9

Handbook of Petrology

Printed at:

Shree Balaji Art Press

Delhi

Preface

Petrology is the branch of geology that studies rocks, and the conditions in which rocks form.

Lithology was once approximately synonymous with petrography, but in current usage, lithology focuses on macroscopic hand-sample or outcrop-scale description of rocks, while petrography is the speciality that deals with microscopic details.

In the oil industry, lithology, or more specifically mud logging, is the graphic representation of geological formations being drilled through, and drawn on a log called a mud log. As the cuttings are circulated out of the borehole they are sampled, examined (typically under a 10x microscope) and tested chemically when needed.

Petrology utilizes the classical fields of mineralogy, petrography, optical mineralogy, and chemical analyses to describe the composition and texture of rocks. Modern petrologists also include the principles of geochemistry and geophysics through the studies of geochemical trends and cycles and the use of thermodynamic data and experiments to better understand the origins of rocks.

There are three branches of petrology, corresponding to the three types of rocks: igneous, metamorphic, and sedimentary, and another dealing with experimental techniques:

- Igneous petrology focuses on the composition and texture of igneous rocks (rocks such as granite or basalt which have crystallized from molten rock or magma). Igneous rocks include volcanic and plutonic rocks.
- Sedimentary petrology focuses on the composition and texture of sedimentary rocks (rocks such as sandstone, shale, or limestone which consist of pieces or particles derived from other rocks or biological or chemical deposits, and are usually bound together in a matrix of finer material).
- Metamorphic petrology focuses on the composition and texture of metamorphic rocks (rocks such as slate, marble, gneiss, or schist which started out as sedimentary or igneous rocks but which have undergone chemical, mineralogical or textural changes due to extremes of pressure, temperature or both).
- Experimental petrology employs high-pressure, high-temperature apparatus to investigate the geochemistry and phase relations of natural or synthetic materials at elevated pressures and temperatures. Experiments are particularly useful for investigating rocks of the lower crust and upper mantle that rarely survive the journey to the surface in pristine condition. The work of experimental petrologists has laid a foundation on which modern understanding of igneous and metamorphic processes has been built.

Author

Contents

1 Introduction

Petrology (from Greek:, *petra*, rock; and , *logos*, knowledge) is the branch of geology that studies rocks, and the conditions in which rocks form.

Lithology was once approximately synonymous with petrography, but in current usage, lithology focuses on macroscopic hand-sample or outcrop-scale description of rocks, while petrography is the speciality that deals with microscopic details.

In the oil industry, lithology, or more specifically mud logging, is the graphic representation of geological formations being drilled through, and drawn on a log called a mud log. As the cuttings are circulated out of the borehole they are sampled, examined (typically under a 10x microscope) and tested chemically when needed.

Petrology utilizes the classical fields of mineralogy, petrography, optical mineralogy, and chemical analyses to describe the composition and texture of rocks. Modern petrologists also include the principles of geochemistry and geophysics through the studies of geochemical trends and cycles and the use of thermodynamic data and experiments to better understand the origins of rocks.

Branches

There are three branches of petrology, corresponding to the three types of rocks: igneous, metamorphic, and sedimentary, and another dealing with experimental techniques:

- Igneous petrology focuses on the composition and texture of igneous rocks (rocks such as granite or basalt which have crystallized from molten rock or magma). Igneous rocks include volcanic and plutonic rocks.
- Sedimentary petrology focuses on the composition and texture of sedimentary rocks (rocks such as sandstone, shale, or limestone which consist of pieces or particles derived from other rocks or biological or chemical deposits, and are usually bound together in a matrix of finer material).
- Metamorphic petrology focuses on the composition and texture of metamorphic rocks (rocks such as slate, marble, gneiss, or schist which started out as sedimentary or igneous rocks but which have undergone chemical, mineralogical or textural changes due to extremes of pressure, temperature or both)
- Experimental petrology employs high-pressure, high-temperature apparatus to investigate the geochemistry and phase relations of natural or synthetic materials at elevated pressures and temperatures. Experiments are particularly useful for investigating rocks of the lower crust and upper mantle that rarely survive the journey to the surface in pristine condition. The work of experimental petrologists has laid a foundation on which modern understanding of igneous and metamorphic processes has been built.

Petrography is a branch of petrology that focuses on detailed descriptions of rocks. Someone who studies petrography is called a petrographer. The mineral content and the textural relationships within the rock are described in detail. Petrographic descriptions start with the field notes at the outcrop and include megascopic description of hand specimens. However, the most important tool for the petrographer is the petrographic microscope. The detailed analysis of minerals by optical mineralogy in thin section and the micro-texture and structure are critical to understanding the origin of the rock. Electron microprobe analysis of individual grains as well as whole rock chemical analysis by atomic absorption or X-ray fluorescence are used in a modern petrographic lab. Individual mineral grains from a rock sample may also be analyzed by X-ray diffraction when optical means are insufficient. Analysis of microscopic fluid inclusions within mineral grains with a heating stage on a petrographic microscope provides clues to the temperature and pressure conditions existent during the mineral formation.

The macroscopic characters of rocks, those visible in hand-specimens without the aid of the microscope, are very varied and difficult to describe accurately and fully. The geologist in the field depends principally on them and on a few rough chemical and physical tests; and to the practical engineer, architect and quarry-master they are all-important. Although frequently insufficient in themselves to determine the true nature of a rock, they usually serve for a preliminary classification, and often give all the information needed.

With a small bottle of acid to test for carbonate of lime, a knife to ascertain the hardness of rocks and minerals, and a pocket lens to magnify their structure, the field geologist is rarely at a loss to what group a rock belongs. The fine grained species are often indeterminable in this way, and the minute mineral components of all rocks can usually be ascertained only by microscopic examination. But it is easy to see that a sandstone or grit consists of more or less rounded, water-worn sand grains and if it contains dull, weathered particles of feldspar, shining scales of mica or small crystals of calcite these also rarely escape observation. Shales and clay rocks generally are soft, fine grained, often laminated and not infrequently contain minute organisms or fragments of plants. Limestones are easily marked with a knife-blade, effervesce readily with weak cold acid and often contain entire or broken shells or other fossils. The crystalline nature of a granite or basalt is obvious at a glance, and while the former contains white or pink feldspar, clear vitreous quartz and glancing flakes of mica, the other shows yellow-green olivine, black augite, and gray stratiated plagioclase.

Other simple tools include the blowpipe (to test the fusibility of detached crystals), the goniometer, the magnet, the magnifying glass and the specific gravity balance.

When dealing with unfamiliar types or with rocks so fine grained that their component minerals cannot be determined with the aid of a hand lens, a microscope is used. Characteristics observed under the microscope include colour, colour variation under plane polarised light (pleochroism, produced by the lower Nicol prism, or more recently polarising films), fracture characteristics of the grains, refractive index (in comparison to the mounting adhesive, typically Canada Balsam), and optical symmetry (birefringent or isotropic). *In toto*, these characteristics are sufficient to identify the mineral, and often to quite tightly estimate its major element composition. The process of identifying minerals under the microscope is fairly subtle, but also mechanistic — it would be possible to develop an identification key that would allow a computer to do it. The more difficult and skilful part of optical petrography is identifying the interrelationships between grains and relating them to features seen in hand specimen, at outcrop, or in mapping. Separation of components.

Separation of the ingredients of a crushed rock powder to obtain pure samples for analysis is a common approach. It may be performed with a powerful, adjustable-strength electromagnet. A weak magnetic field attracts magnetite, then haematite and other iron ores. Silicates that contain iron follow in definite order–biotite, enstatite, augite, hornblende, garnet, and similar ferro-magnesian minerals are successively abstracted. Finally, only the colourless, non-magnetic compounds, such as muscovite, calcite, quartz, and feldspar remain. Chemical methods also are useful.

A weak acid dissolves calcite from crushed limestone, leaving only dolomite, silicates, or quartz. Hydrofluoric acid attacks feldspar before quartz and, if used cautiously, dissolves these and any glassy material in a rock powder before it dissolves augite or hypersthene.

Methods of separation by specific gravity have a still wider application. The simplest of these is levigation–treatment by a current of water. Levigationis extensively employed in mechanical analysis of soils and treatment of ores, but is not so successful with rocks, as their components do not, as a rule, differ greatly in specific gravity. Fluids are used that do not attack most rock-forming minerals, but have a high specific gravity. Solutions of potassium mercuric iodide (sp. gr. 3.196), cadmium borotungstate (sp. gr. 3.30), methylene iodide (sp. gr. 3.32), bromoform (sp. gr. 2.86), or acetylene bromide (sp. gr. 3.00) are the principal fluids employed. They may be diluted (with water, benzene, etc.) or concentrated by evaporation.

If the rock is granite consisting of biotite (sp. gr. 3.1), muscovite (sp. gr. 2.85), quartz (sp. gr. 2.65), oligoclase (sp. gr. 2.64), and orthoclase (sp. gr. 2.56), the crushed minerals float in methylene iodide. On gradual dilution with benzene they precipitate in the order above. Simple in theory, these methods are tedious in practice, especially as it is common for one rock-making mineral to enclose another. However, expert handling of fresh and suitable rocks yields excellent results.

Chemical Analysis

In addition to naked-eye and microscopic investigation, chemical research methods of are of great practical importance to the petrographer. Crushed and separated powders, obtained by the processes above, may be analyzed to determine chemical composition of minerals in the rock qualitatively or quantitatively. Chemical testing, and microscopic examination of minute grains is an elegant and valuable means of discriminating between mineral components of fine-grained rocks.

Thus, the presence of apatite in rock-sections is established by covering a bare rock-section with ammonium molybdate solution. A turbid yellow precipitate forms over the crystals of the mineral in question (indicating the presence of phosphates). Many silicates are insoluble in acids and cannot be tested in this way, but others are partly dissolved, leaving a film of gelatinous silica that can be stained with colouring matters, such as the aniline dyes (nepheline, analcite, zeolites, etc.)

Complete chemical analysis of rocks are also widely used and important, especially in describing new species. Rock analysis has of late years (largely under the influence of the chemical laboratory of the United States Geological Survey) reached a high pitch of refinement and complexity. As many as twenty or twenty-five components may be determined, but for practical purposes a knowledge of the relative proportions of silica, alumina, ferrous and ferric oxides, magnesia, lime, potash, soda and water carry us a long way in determining a rock's position in the conventional classifications.

A chemical analysis is usually sufficient to indicate whether a rock is igneous or sedimentary, and in either case to accurately show what subdivision of these classes it belongs to. In the case of metamorphic rocks it often establishes whether the original mass was a sediment or of volcanic origin.

Specific Gravity

Specific gravity of rocks is determined by means of a balance and pycnometer. It is greatest in rocks with the most magnesia, iron, and heavy metals—least in rocks rich in alkalis, silica, and water. It diminishes with weathering and, generally, highly crystalline rocks have higher specific gravity than wholly or partly vitreous rocks of the same chemical composition. The specific gravity of the commoner rocks ranges from about 2.5 to 3.2.

Archaeological Applications

Archaeologists use petrography to identify mineral components in pottery. This information ties the artifacts to geological source areas for the clay used and the rock fragments (usually called 'temper' or 'aplastics') potters often add to modify the clay's properties. This provides insight into how potters selected and used local and non-local resources, and helps archaeologists determine whether pottery found in a particular location was locally produced or traded from elsewhere. In turn, this kind of information (in combination with other evidence) can support inferences about settlement patterns, group and individual mobility, and social contacts or trade networks. In addition, an understanding of how certain minerals are altered at specific temperatures can allow archaeological petrographers to infer aspects of the ceramic production process itself, such as minimum and maximum temperatures reached in the original firing of the pot.

2 Volcano

A volcano is an opening, or rupture, in a planet's surface or crust, which allows hot magma, volcanic ash and gases to escape from below the surface.

Volcanoes are generally found where tectonic plates are diverging or converging. A mid-oceanic ridge, for example the Mid-Atlantic Ridge, has examples of volcanoes caused by divergent tectonic plates pulling apart; the Pacific Ring of Fire has examples of volcanoes caused by convergent tectonic plates coming together. By contrast, volcanoes are usually not created where two tectonic plates slide past one another. Volcanoes can also form where there is stretching and thinning of the Earth's crust (called 'non-hotspot intraplate volcanism'), such as in the East African Rift, the Wells Gray-Clearwater volcanic field and the Rio Grande Rift in North America.

Volcanoes can be caused by mantle plumes. These so-called hotspots, for example at Hawaii, can occur far from plate boundaries. Hotspot volcanoes are also found elsewhere in the solar system, especially on rocky planets and moons.

At the mid-oceanic ridges, two tectonic plates diverge from one another. New oceanic crust is being formed by hot molten rock slowly cooling and solidifying. The crust is very thin at mid-oceanic ridges due to the pull of the tectonic plates. The release of pressure due to the thinning of the crust leads to adiabatic expansion, and the partial melting of the mantle causing volcanism and creating new oceanic crust. Most divergent plate boundaries are at the bottom of the oceans, therefore most volcanic activity is submarine, forming new seafloor. Black smokers or deep sea vents are an example of this kind of volcanic activity. Where the mid-oceanic ridge is above sea-level, volcanic islands are formed, for example, Iceland.

Subduction zones are places where two plates, usually an oceanic plate and a continental plate, collide. In this case, the oceanic plate subducts, or submerges under the continental plate forming a deep ocean trench just offshore. Water released from the subducting plate lowers the melting temperature of the overlying mantle wedge, creating magma. This magma tends to be very viscous due to its high silica content, so often does not reach the surface and cools at depth. When it does reach the surface, a volcano is formed. Typical examples for this kind of volcano are Mount Etna and the volcanoes in the Pacific Ring of Fire.

Hotspots

Hotspots are not usually located on the ridges of tectonic plates, but above mantle plumes, where the convection of the Earth's mantle creates a column of hot material that rises until it reaches the crust, which tends to be thinner than in other areas of the Earth. The temperature of the plume causes the crust to melt and form pipes, which can vent magma. Because the tectonic plates move whereas the mantle plume remains in the same place, each volcano becomes dormant after a while and a new volcano is then formed as the plate shifts over the hotspot. The Hawaiian Islands are thought to be formed in such a manner, as well as the Snake River Plain, with the Yellowstone Caldera being the part of the North American plate currently above the hot spot.

The most common perception of a volcano is of a conical mountain, spewing lava and poisonous gases from a crater at its summit. This describes just one of many types of volcano, and the features of volcanoes are much more complicated. The structure and behaviour of volcanoes depends on a number of factors. Some volcanoes have rugged peaks formed by lava domes rather than a summit crater, whereas others present landscape features such as massive plateaus. Vents that issue volcanic material (lava, which is what magma is called once it has escaped to the surface, and ash) and gases (mainly steam and magmatic gases) can be located anywhere on the landform. Many of these vents give rise to smaller cones such as Pu u on a flank of Hawaii's Kilauea.

Other types of volcano include cryovolcanoes (or ice volcanoes), particularly on some moons of Jupiter, Saturn and Neptune; and mud volcanoes, which are formations often not associated with known magmatic activity. Active mud volcanoes tend to involve temperatures much lower than those of igneous volcanoes, except when a mud volcano is actually a vent of an igneous volcano.

Shield Volcanoes

Shield volcanoes, so named for their broad, shield-like profiles, are formed by the eruption of low-viscosity lava that can flow a great distance from a vent, but not generally explode catastrophically. Since low-viscosity magma is typically low in silica, shield volcanoes are more common in oceanic than continental settings. The Hawaiian volcanic chain is a series of shield cones, and they are common in Iceland, as well.

Lava Domes

Lava domes are built by slow eruptions of highly viscous lavas. They are sometimes formed within the crater of a previous volcanic eruption (as in Mount Saint Helens), but can also form independently, as in the case of Lassen

Peak. Like stratovolcanoes, they can produce violent, explosive eruptions, but their lavas generally do not flow far from the originating vent.

Cryptodomes

Cryptodomes are formed when viscous lava forces its way up and causes a bulge. The 1980 eruption of Mount St. Helens was an example. Lava was under great pressure and forced a bulge in the mountain, which was unstable and slid down the north side.

Volcanic Cones (Cinder Cones)

Volcanic cones or cinder cones are the result from eruptions that erupt mostly small pieces of scoria and pyroclastics (both resemble cinders, hence the name of this volcano type) that build up around the vent. These can be relatively short-lived eruptions that produce a cone-shaped hill perhaps 30 to 400 metres high. Most cinder cones erupt only once. Cinder cones may form as flank vents on larger volcanoes, or occur on their own. Parícutin in Mexico and Sunset Crater in Arizona are examples of cinder cones. In New Mexico, Caja del Rio is a volcanic field of over 60 cinder cones.

Stratovolcanoes (Composite Volcanoes)

Stratovolcanoes or composite volcanoes are tall conical mountains composed of lava flows and other ejecta in alternate layers, the strata that give rise to the name. Stratovolcanoes are also known as composite volcanoes, created from several structures during different kinds of eruptions. Strato/composite volcanoes are made of cinders, ash and lava. Cinders and ash pile on top of each other, lava flows on top of the ash, where it cools and hardens, and then the process begins again. Classic examples include Mt. Fuji in Japan, Mayon Volcano in the Philippines, and Mount Vesuvius and Stromboli in Italy.

In recorded history, explosive eruptions by stratovolcanoes have posed the greatest hazard to civilizations, as ash is produced by an explosive eruption. No supervolcano erupted in recorded history. Shield volcanoes have not an enormous pressure build up from the lava flow. Fissure vents and monogenetic volcanic fields (volcanic cones) have not powerful explosive eruptions, as they are many times under extension. Stratovolcanoes (30-35°) are steeper than shield volcanoes (generally 5-10°), their lose tephra are material for dangerous lahars.

Supervolcanoes

A supervolcano is a large volcano that usually has a large caldera and can potentially produce devastation on an enormous, sometimes continental, scale. Such eruptions would be able to cause severe cooling of global temperatures for many years afterwards because of the huge volumes of sulfur and ash erupted. They are the most dangerous type of volcano. Examples include Yellowstone Caldera in Yellowstone National Park and Valles Caldera in New Mexico (both western United States), Lake Taupo in New Zealand, Lake Toba in Sumatra, Indonesia and Ngorogoro Crater in Tanzania. Supervolcanoes are hard to identify centuries later, given the enormous areas they cover. Large igneous provinces are also considered supervolcanoes because of the vast amount of basalt lava erupted, but are non-explosive.

Submarine Volcanoes

Submarine volcanoes are common features on the ocean floor. Some are active and, in shallow water, disclose their presence by blasting steam and rocky debris high above the surface of the sea. Many others lie at such great depths that the tremendous weight of the water above them prevents the explosive release of steam and gases, although they can be detected by hydrophones and discolouration of water because of volcanic gases. Pumice rafts may also appear. Even large submarine eruptions may not disturb the ocean surface. Because of the rapid cooling effect of water as compared to air, and increased buoyancy, submarine volcanoes often form rather steep pillars over their volcanic vents as compared to above-surface volcanoes. They may become so large that they break the ocean surface as new islands. Pillow lava is a common eruptive product of submarine volcanoes. Hydrothermal vents are common near these volcanoes, and some support peculiar ecosystems based on dissolved minerals.

Subglacial Volcanoes

Subglacial volcanoes develop underneath icecaps. They are made up of flat lava which flows at the top of extensive pillow lavas and palagonite. When the icecap melts, the lavas on the top collapse, leaving a flat-topped mountain. These volcanoes are also called table mountains, tuyas or (uncommonly) mobergs. Very good examples of this type of volcano can be seen in Iceland, however, there are also tuyas in British Columbia. The origin of the term comes from Tuya Butte, which is one of the several tuyas in the area of the Tuya River and Tuya Range in northern British Columbia. Tuya Butte was the first such landform analyzed and so its name has entered the geological literature for this kind of volcanic formation. The Tuya Mountains Provincial Park was recently established to protect this unusual landscape, which lies north of Tuya Lake and south of the Jennings River near the boundary with the Yukon Territory.

Lava Composition

Another way of classifying volcanoes is by the *composition of material erupted* (lava), since this affects the shape of the volcano. Lava can be broadly classified into four different compositions:

1. If the erupted magma contains a high percentage (>63%) of silica, the lava is called felsic.

2. Felsic lavas (dacites or rhyolites) tend to be highly viscous (not very fluid) and are erupted as domes or short, stubby flows. Viscous lavas tend to form stratovolcanoes or lava domes. Lassen Peak in California is an example of a volcano formed from felsic lava and is actually a large lava dome.

3. Because siliceous magmas are so viscous, they tend to trap volatiles (gases) that are present, which cause the magma to erupt catastrophically, eventually forming stratovolcanoes. Pyroclastic flows (ignimbrites) are highly hazardous products of such volcanoes, since they are composed of molten volcanic ash too heavy to go up into the atmosphere, so they hug the volcano's slopes and travel far from their vents during large eruptions. Temperatures as high as 1,200° C are known to occur in pyroclastic flows, which will incinerate everything flammable in their path and thick layers of hot pyroclastic flow deposits can be laid down, often up to many metres thick. Alaska's Valley of Ten Thousand Smokes, formed by the eruption of Novarupta near Katmai in 1912, is an example of a thick pyroclastic flow or ignimbrite deposit. Volcanic ash that is light enough to be erupted high into the Earth's atmosphere may travel many kilometres before it falls back to ground as a tuff.

4. If the erupted magma contains 52-63 per cent silica, the lava is of *intermediate* composition.

These 'andesitic' volcanoes generally only occur above subduction zones (e.g. Mount Merapi in Indonesia).

Andesitic lava is typically formed at convergent boundary margins of tectonic plates, by several processes:

- Hydration melting of peridotite and fractional crystallization
- Melting of subducted slab containing sediments

- Magma mixing between felsic rhyolitic and mafic basaltic magmas in an intermediate reservoir prior to emplacement or lava flow.
- If the erupted magma contains <52 per cent and >45 per cent silica, the lava is called mafic (because it contains higher percentages of magnesium (Mg) and iron (Fe)) or basaltic. These lavas are usually much less viscous than rhyolitic lavas, depending on their eruption temperature; they also tend to be hotter than felsic lavas. Mafic lavas occur in a wide range of settings.
- At mid-ocean ridges, where two oceanic plates are pulling apart, basaltic lava erupts as pillows to fill the gap.
- Shield volcanoes (e.g. the Hawaiian Islands, including Mauna Loa and Kilauea), on both oceanic and continental crust;
- As continental flood basalts.

Some erupted magmas contain <=45 per cent silica and produce ultramafic lava. Ultramafic flows, also known as komatiites, are very rare; indeed, very few have been erupted at the Earth's surface since the Proterozoic, when the planet's heat flow was higher. They are (or were) the hottest lavas, and probably more fluid than common mafic lavas.

Lava Texture

Two types of lava are named according to the surface texture: A a (pronounced and pahoehoe both Hawaiian words. ?A?a is characterized by a rough, clinkery surface and is the typical texture of viscous lava flows. However, even basaltic or mafic flows can be erupted as ?a?a flows, particularly if the eruption rate is high and the slope is steep.

Pahoehoe is characterized by its smooth and often ropey or wrinkly surface and is generally formed from more fluid lava flows. Usually, only mafic flows will erupt as pahoehoe, since they often erupt at higher temperatures or have the proper chemical make-up to allow them to flow with greater fluidity.

A popular way of classifying magmatic volcanoes is by their frequency of eruption, with those that erupt regularly called active, those that have erupted in historical *times* but are now quiet called dormant, and those that have not erupted in historical times called extinct. However, these popular classifications—extinct in particular—are practically meaningless to scientists. They use classifications which refer to a particular volcano's formative and eruptive processes and resulting shapes, which was explained above.

There is no real consensus among volcanologists on how to define an 'active' volcano. The lifespan of a volcano can vary from months to several million years, making such a distinction sometimes meaningless when compared to the lifespans of humans or even civilizations. For example, many of Earth's volcanoes have erupted dozens of times in the past few thousand years but are not currently showing signs of eruption. Given the long lifespan of such volcanoes, they are very active. By human lifespans, however, they are not.

Scientists usually consider a volcano to be erupting or likely to erupt if it is currently erupting, or showing signs of unrest such as unusual earthquake activity or significant new gas emissions. Most scientists consider a volcano *active* if it has erupted in holocene times. Historic times is another timeframe for *active*. But it is important to note that the span of recorded history differs from region to region. In China and the Mediterranean, recorded history reaches back more than 3,000 years but in the Pacific Northwest of the United States and Canada, it reaches back less than 300 years, and in Hawaii and New Zealand, only around 200 years. The Smithsonian Global Volcanism Programme's definition of *active* is having erupted within the last 10,000 years (the 'holocene' period).

Presently there are about 500 active volcanoes in the world — the majority following along the Pacific 'Ring of Fire' — and around 50 of these erupt each year. The United States is home to 50 active volcanoes There are more than 1,500 potentially active volcanoes. An estimated 500 million people live near active volcanoes.

Extinct

Extinct volcanoes are those that scientists consider unlikely to erupt again, because the volcano no longer has a lava supply. Examples of extinct volcanoes are many volcanoes on the Hawaiian — Emperor seamount chain in the Pacific Ocean (extinct because the Hawaii hotspot is centered near the Big Island), Hohentwiel, Shiprock, and Paricutin (which is monogenetic). Otherwise, whether a volcano is truly extinct is often difficult to determine. Since 'supervolcano' calderas can have eruptive lifespans sometimes measured in millions of years, a caldera that has not produced an eruption in tens of thousands of years is likely to be considered dormant instead of extinct.

Dormant

It is difficult to distinguish an extinct volcano from a dormant one. Volcanoes are often considered to be extinct if there are no written records of its activity. Nevertheless volcanoes may remain dormant for a long period of time, Yellowstone has a repose/recharge period of around 700 ka and Toba of around 380 ka. Vesuvius was described by Roman writers as having been covered with gardens and vineyards before its famous eruption of AD 79, which destroyed the towns of Herculaneum and Pompeii. Before the catastrophic eruption of 1991, Pinatubo was an inconspicuous volcano, unknown to most people in the surrounding areas. More recently, the long-dormant Soufrière Hills volcano on the island of Montserrat was thought to be extinct before activity resumed in 1995. Another recent example is Fourpeaked Mountain in Alaska, which, prior to its eruption in September 2006, had not erupted since before 8000 BC and was long thought to be extinct.

There are many different types of volcanic eruptions and associated activity: phreatic eruptions (steam-generated eruptions), explosive eruption of high-silica lava (e.g., rhyolite), effusive eruption of low-silica lava (e.g., basalt), pyroclastic flows, lahars (debris flow) and carbon dioxide emission. All of these activities can pose a hazard to humans. Earthquakes, hot springs, fumaroles, mud pots and geysers often accompany volcanic activity.

The concentrations of different volcanic gases can vary considerably from one volcano to the next. Water vapour is typically the most abundant volcanic gas, followed by carbon dioxide and sulfur dioxide. Other principal volcanic gases include hydrogen sulfide, hydrogen chloride, and hydrogen fluoride. A large number of minor and trace gases are also found in volcanic emissions, for example hydrogen, carbon monoxide, halocarbons, organic compounds, and volatile metal chlorides.

Large, explosive volcanic eruptions inject water vapour (H_2O), carbon dioxide (CO_2), sulfur dioxide (SO_2), hydrogen chloride (HCl), hydrogen fluoride (HF) and ash (pulverized rock and pumice) into the stratosphere to heights of 16-32 kilometres (10-20 mi) above the Earth's surface. The most significant impacts from these injections come from the conversion of sulfur dioxide to sulfuric acid (H_2SO_4), which condenses rapidly in the stratosphere to form fine sulfate aerosols. The aerosols increase the Earth's albedo—its reflection of radiation from the Sun back into space — and thus cool the Earth's lower atmosphere or troposphere; however, they also absorb heat radiated up from the Earth, thereby warming the stratosphere. Several eruptions during the past century have caused a decline in the average temperature at the Earth's surface of up to half a degree (Fahrenheit scale) for periods of one to three years — sulfur dioxide from the eruption of Huaynaputina probably caused the Russian famine of 1601-1603.

One proposed volcanic winter happened c. 70,000 years ago following the supereruption of Lake Toba on Sumatra island in Indonesia. According to the Toba catastrophe theory to which some anthropologists and archeologists subscribe, it had global consequences, killing most humans then alive and creating a population bottleneck that affected the genetic inheritance of all humans today. The 1815 eruption of Mount Tambora created global climate anomalies that became known as the 'Year Without a Summer' because of the effect on North American and European weather. Agricultural crops failed and livestock died in much of the Northern Hemisphere, resulting in one of the worst famines of the 19th century. The freezing winter of 1740-41, which led to widespread famine in northern Europe, may also owe its origins to a volcanic eruption.

It has been suggested that volcanic activity caused or contributed to the End-Ordovician, Permian-Triassic, Late Devonian mass extinctions, and possibly others. The massive eruptive event which formed the Siberian Traps, one of the largest known volcanic events of the last 500 million years of Earth's geological history, continued for a million years and is considered to be the likely cause of the 'Great Dying' about 250 million years ago, which is estimated to have killed 90 per cent of species existing at the time.

The sulfate aerosols also promote complex chemical reactions on their surfaces that alter chlorine and nitrogen chemical species in the stratosphere. This effect, together with increased stratospheric chlorine levels from chlorofluorocarbon pollution, generates chlorine monoxide (ClO), which destroys ozone (O_3). As the aerosols grow and coagulate, they settle down into the upper troposphere where they serve as nuclei for cirrus clouds and further modify the Earth's radiation balance. Most of the hydrogen chloride (HCl) and hydrogen fluoride (HF) are dissolved in water droplets in the eruption cloud and quickly fall to the ground as acid rain. The injected ash also falls rapidly from the stratosphere; most of it is removed within several days to a few weeks. Finally, explosive volcanic eruptions release the greenhouse gas carbon dioxide and thus provide a deep source of carbon for biogeochemical cycles.

Gas emissions from volcanoes are a natural contributor to acid rain. Volcanic activity releases about 130 to 230 teragrams (145 million to 255 million short tons) of carbon dioxide each year. Volcanic eruptions may inject aerosols into the Earth's atmosphere. Large injections may cause visual effects such as unusually colourful sunsets and affect global climate mainly by cooling it. Volcanic eruptions also provide the benefit of adding nutrients to soil through the weathering process of volcanic rocks. These fertile soils assist the growth of plants and various crops. Volcanic eruptions can also create new islands, as the magma cools and solidifies upon contact with the water.

Ash thrown into the air by eruptions can present a hazard to aircraft, especially jet aircraft where the particles can be melted by the high operating temperature. Dangerous encounters in 1982 after the eruption of Galunggung in Indonesia, and 1989 after the eruption of Mount Redoubt in Alaska raised awareness of this phenomenon. Nine Volcanic Ash Advisory Centres were established by the International Civil Aviation Organization to monitor ash clouds and advise pilots accordingly. The 2010 eruptions of Eyjafjallajökull caused major disruptions to air travel in Europe.

The Earth's Moon has no large volcanoes and no current volcanic activity, although recent evidence suggests it may still possess a partially molten core. However, the Moon does have many volcanic features such as maria (the darker patches seen on the moon), rilles and domes.

The planet Venus has a surface that is 90 per cent basalt, indicating that volcanism played a major role in shaping its surface. The planet may have had a major global resurfacing event about 500 million years ago, from what scientists can tell from the density of impact craters on the surface. Lava flows are widespread and forms of volcanism not present on Earth occur as well. Changes in the planet's atmosphere and observations of lightning have been attributed to ongoing volcanic eruptions, although there is no confirmation of whether or not Venus is still volcanically active. However, radar sounding by the Magellan probe revealed evidence for comparatively recent volcanic activity at Venus's highest volcano Maat Mons, in the form of ash flows near the summit and on the northern flank.

There are several extinct volcanoes on Mars, four of which are vast shield volcanoes far bigger than any on Earth. They include Arsia Mons, Ascraeus Mons, Hecates Tholus, Olympus Mons, and Pavonis Mons. These volcanoes have been extinct for many millions of years, but the European *Mars Express* spacecraft has found evidence that volcanic activity may have occurred on Mars in the recent past as well.

Jupiter's moon Io is the most volcanically active object in the solar system because of tidal interaction with Jupiter. It is covered with volcanoes that erupt sulfur, sulfur dioxide and silicate rock, and as a result, Io is constantly being resurfaced. Its lavas are the hottest known anywhere in the solar system, with temperatures exceeding 1,800 K (1,500° C). In February 2001, the largest recorded volcanic eruptions in the solar system occurred on Io. Europa, the smallest of Jupiter's Galilean moons, also appears to have an active volcanic system, except that its volcanic activity is entirely in the form of water, which freezes into ice on the frigid surface. This process is known as cryovolcanism, and is apparently most common on the moons of the outer planets of the solar system.

In 1989 the Voyager 2 spacecraft observed cryovolcanoes (ice volcanoes) on Triton, a moon of Neptune, and in 2005 the Cassini-Huygens probe photographed fountains of frozen particles erupting from Enceladus, a moon of Saturn. The ejecta may be composed of water, liquid nitrogen, dust, or methane compounds. Cassini-Huygens also found evidence of a methane-spewing cryovolcano on the Saturnian moon Titan, which is believed to be a significant source of the methane found in its atmosphere. It is theorized that cryovolcanism may also be present on the Kuiper Belt Object Quaoar.

A 2010 study of the exoplanet COROT-7b, which was detected by transit in 2009, studied that tidal heating from the host star very close to the planet and neighbouring planets could generate intense volcanic activity similar to Io.

Traditional Beliefs About Volcanoes

Many ancient accounts ascribe volcanic eruptions to supernatural causes, such as the actions of gods or demigods. To the ancient Greeks, volcanoes' capricious power could only be explained as acts of the gods, while 16th/17th-century German astronomer Johannes Kepler believed they were ducts for the Earth's tears. One early idea counter to this was proposed by Jesuit Athanasius Kircher (1602-1680), who witnessed eruptions of Mount Etna and Stromboli, then visited the crater of Vesuvius and published his view of an Earth with a central fire connected to numerous others caused by the burning of sulfur, bitumen and coal.

Various explanations were proposed for volcano behaviour before the modern understanding of the Earth's mantle structure as a semisolid material was developed. For decades after awareness that compression and radioactive materials may be heat sources, their contributions were specifically discounted. Volcanic action was often attributed to chemical reactions and a thin layer of molten rock near the surface.

During a volcanic eruption, lava, tephra (ash, lapilli, volcanic bombs and blocks), and various gases are expelled from a volcanic vent or fissure. Several types of volcanic eruptions have been distinguished by volcanologists. These are often named after famous volcanoes where that type of behaviour has been observed. Some volcanoes may exhibit only one characteristic type of eruption during a period of activity, while others may display an entire sequence of types all in one eruptive series.

There are three different metatypes of eruptions. The most well-observed are magmatic eruptions, which involve the decompression of gas within magma that propels it forward. Phreatomagmatic eruptions are another type of volcanic eruption, driven by a the compression of gas within magma, the direct opposite of the process powering magmatic activity. The last eruptive metatype is the Phreatic eruption, which is driven by the superheating of steam via contact with magma; these eruptive types often exhibit no magmatic release, instead causing the granulation of existing rock.

Within these wide-defining eruptive types are several subtypes. The weakest are Hawaiian and submarine, then Strombolian, followed by Vulcanian and Surtseyan. The stronger eruptive types are Pelean eruptions, followed by Plinian eruptions; the strongest eruptions are called 'Ultra Plinian'. Subglacial and Phreatic eruptions are defined by their eruptive mechanism, and vary in strength. An important measure of erruptive strength is Volcanic Explosivity Index (VEI), a magnitudic scale ranging from 0 to 8 that often correlates to eruptive types.

Volcanic eruptions arise through three main mechanisms:

1. Gas release under decompression causing magmatic eruptions.
2. Thermal contraction from chilling on contact with water causing phreatomagmatic eruptions.

3. Ejection of entrained particles during steam eruptions causing phreatic eruptions.

There are two types of eruptions in terms of activity, explosive eruptions and effusive eruptions. Explosive eruptions are characterized by gas-driven explosions that propels magma and tephra. Effusive eruptions, meanwhile, are characterized by the outpouring of lava without significant explosive eruption.

Volcanic eruptions vary widely in strength. On the one extreme there are effusive Hawaiian eruptions, which are characterized by lava fountains and fluid lava flows, which are typically not very dangerous. On the other extreme, Plinian eruptions are large, violent, and highly dangerous explosive events. Volcanoes are not bound to one eruptive style, and frequently display many different types, both passive and explosive, even the span of a single eruptive cycle. Volcanoes do not always erupt vertically from a single crater near their peak, either. Some volcanoes exhibit lateral and fissure eruptions. Notably, many Hawaiian eruptions start from rift zones, and some of the strongest Surtseyan eruptions develop along fracture zones.

Hawaiian eruptions are a type of volcanic eruption, named after the Hawaiian volcanoes with which this eruptive type is hallmark. Hawaiian eruptions are the calmest types of volcanic events, characterized by the effusive eruption eruption of very fluid basalt-type lavas with low gaseous content. The volume of ejected material from Hawaiian eruptions is less than half of that found in other eruptive types. Steady production of small amounts of lava builds up the large, broad form of a shield volcano. Eruptions are not centralized at the main summit as with other volcanic types, and often occur at vents around the summit and from fissure vents radiating out of the centre.

Hawaiian eruptions often begin as a line of vent eruptions along a fissure vent, a so-called 'curtain of fire'.

These die down as the lava beings to concentrate at a few of the vents. Central-vent eruptions, meanwhile, often take the form of large lava fountains (both continuous and sporadic), which can reach heights of hundreds of meters or more. The particles from lava fountains usually cool in the air before hitting the ground, resulting in the accumulation of cindery scoria fragments; however, when the air is especially thick with clasts, they cannot cool off fast enough due to the surrounding heat, and hit the ground still hot, the accumulation of which forms splatter cones. If eruptive rates are high enough, they may even form splatter-fed lava flows. Hawaiian eruptions are often extremely long lived; Pu'u O'o, a cinder cone of Kilauea, has been erupting continuously since 1983. Another Hawaiian volcanic feature is the formation of active lava lakes, self-maintaining pools of raw lava with a thin crust of semi-cooled rock; there are currently only five such lakes in the world, and the one at Kilauea's Kupaianaha vent is one of them.

Flows from Hawaiian eruptions are basaltic, and can be divided into two types by their structural characteristics. Pahoehoe lava is a relatively smooth lava flow that can be billowy or ropey. They can move as one sheet, by the advancement of "toes," or as a snaking lava column. A'a lava flows are denser and more viscous then pahoehoe, but tend to move slower. Flows can measure 2 to 20 m (7 to 66 ft) thick. A'a flows are so thick that the outside layers cools into a rubble-like mass, insulating the still-hot interior and preventing it from cooling. A'a lava moves in a peculiar way–the front of the flow steepens due to pressure from behind until it breaks off, after which the general mass behind it moves forward. Pahoehoe lava can sometimes become A'a lava due to increasing viscosity or increasing rate of shear, but A'a lava never turns into pahoehoe flow.

Hawaiian eruptions are responsible for several unique volcanological objects. Small volcanic particles are carried and formed by the wind, chilling quickly into teardrop-shaped glassy fragments known as Pele's tears (after Pele, the Hawaiian volcano deity). During especially high winds these chunks may even take the form of long drawn out rods, known as Pele's hair. Sometimes basant aerates into reticulite, the lowest density rock type on earth.

Although Hawaiian eruptions are named after the volcanoes of Hawaii, they are not necessarily restricted to them; the largest lava fountain ever recorded formed on the island of Izu Oshima (on Mount Mihara) in 1986, a 1,600 m (5,249 ft) gusher that was more than twice as high as the mountain itself (which stands at 764 m (2,507 ft)).

Volcanoes known to have Hawaiian activity include:

- Pu'u O'o, a parasitic cinder cone located on Kilauea on the island of Hawai?i which has been erupting continuously since 1983. The eruptions began with a 6 km (4 mi)-long fissure-based "curtain of fire" on January 3. These gave way to centralized eruptions on the site of Kilauea's east rift, eventually building up the still active cone.

Strombolian eruptions are a type of volcanic eruption, named after the volcano Stromboli, which has been erupting continuously for centuries. Strombolian eruptions are driven by the bursting of gas bubbles within the magma. These gas bubbles within the magma accumulate and coalesce into large bubbles, called gas slugs. These grow large enough to rise through the lava column. Upon reaching the surface, the difference in air pressure causes the bubble to burst with a loud pop, throwing magma in the air in a way similar to a soap bubble. Because of the high gas pressures associated with the lavas, continued activity is generally in the form of episodic explosive eruptions accompanied by the distinctive loud blasts. During eruptions, these blasts occur as often as every few minutes.

The term 'Strombolian' has been used indiscriminately to describe a wide variety of volcanic eruptions, varying from small volcanic blasts to large eruptive columns. In reality, true Strombolian eruptions are characterized by short-lived and explosive eruptions of lavas with intermediate viscosity, often ejected high into the air. Columns can measure hundreds of metres in height. The lavas formed by Strombolian eruptions are a form of relatively viscous basaltic lava, and its end product is mostly scoria. The relative passivity of Strombolian eruptions, and its non-damaging nature to its source vent allow Strombolian eruptions to continue unabated for thousands of years, and also makes it one of the least dangerous eruptive types.

Strombolian eruptions eject volcanic bombs and lapilli fragments that travel in parabolic paths before landing around their source vent. The steady accumulation of small fragments builds cinder cones composed completely of basaltic pyroclasts. This form of accumulation tends to result in well-ordered rings of tephra.

Strombolian eruptions are similar to Hawaiian eruptions, but there are differences. Strombolian eruptions are noisier, produce no sustained eruptive columns, do not produce some volcanic products associated with Hawaiian volcanism (specifically Pele's tears and Pele's hair), and produce fewer molten lava flows (although the eruptive material does tend to form small rivulets).

Volcanoes known to have Strombolian activity include:

- Parícutin, Mexico, which erupted from a fissure in a cornfield in 1943. Two years into its life, pyroclastic activity began to wane, and the outpouring of lava from its base became its primary mode of activity. Eruptions ceased in 1952, and the final height was 424 m (1,391 ft). This was the first time that scientists are able to observe the complete life cycle of a volcano.

- Mount Etna, Italy, which has displayed Strombolian activity in recent eruptions, for example in 1981, 1999, 2002-2003, and 2009.
- Mount Erebus in Antarctica, the southernmost active volcano in the world, having been observed erupting since 1972. Eruptive activity at Erebrus consists of frequent Strombolian activity.
- Stromboli itself. The namesake of the mild explosive activity that it possesses has been active throughout historical time; essentially continuous Strombolian eruptions, occasionally accompanied by lava flows, have been recorded at Stromboli for more than a millennium.

Vulcanian

Vulcanian eruptions are a type of volcanic eruption, named after the volcano Vulcano, which also gives its name to the word *Volcano.* It was named so following Giuseppe Mercalli's observations of its 1888-1890 eruptions. In Vulcanian eruptions, highly viscous magma within the volcano make it difficult for vesiculate gases to escape. Similar to Strombolian eruptions, this leads to the buildup of high gas pressure, eventually popping the cap holding the magma down and resulting in an explosive eruption. However, unlike Strombolian eruptions, ejected lava fragments are not aerodynamical; this is due to the higher viscosity of Vulcanian magma and the greater incorporation of crystalline material broken off from the former cap. They are also more explosive than their Strombolian counterparts, with eruptive columns often reaching between 5 and 10 kms (3 and 6 mi) high. Lastly, Vulcanian deposits are andesitic to dacitic rather than basaltic.

Initial Vulcanian activity is characterized by a series of short-lived explosions, lasting a few minutes to a few hours and typified by the ejection of volcanic bombs and blocks. These eruptions wear down the lava dome holding the magma down, and it disintegrates, leading to much more quiet and continuous eruptions. Thus an early sign of future

Vulcanian activity is lava dome growth, and its collapse generates an outpouring of pyroclastic material down the volcano's slope.

Deposits near the source vent consist of large volcanic blocks and bombs, with so-called 'bread-crust bombs' being especially common. These deeply cracked volcanic chunks form when the exterior of ejected lava cools quickly into a glassy or fine-grained shell, but the inside continues to cool and vesiculate. The center of the fragment expands, cracking the exterior. However the bulk of Vulcanian deposits are fine grained ash. The ash is only moderately dispersed, and its abundance indicates a high degree of fragmentation, the result of high gas contents within the magma. In some cases these have been found to be the result of interaction with meteoric water, suggesting that Vulcanian eruptions are partially hydrovolcanic.

Peléan eruptions (or nuée ardente) are a type of volcanic eruption, named after the volcano Mount Pelée in Martinique, the site of a massive Peléan eruption in 1902 that is one of the worst natural disasters in history. In Peléan eruptions, a large amount of gas, dust, ash, and lava fragmets are blown out the volcano's central crater, driven by the collapse of rhyolite, dacite, and andesite lava dome collapses that often create large eruptive columns. An early sign of a coming eruption is the growth of a so-called Peléan or lava spine, a bulge in the volcano's summit preempting its total collapse. The material collapses upon itself, forming a fast-moving pyroclastic flow (known as a block-and-ash flow) that moves down the side of the mountain at tremendous speeds, often over 150 kms (93 mi) per hour. These massive landslides make Peléan eruptions one of the most dangerous in the world, capable of tearing through populated areas and causing massive loss of life. The 1902 eruption of Mount Pelée caused tremendous destruction, killing more than 30,000 people and competely destroying the town of St. Pierre, the worst volcanic event in the 20th century.

Peléan eruptions are characterized most prominently by the incandescent pyroclastic flows that they drive. The mechanics of a Peléan eruption are very similar to that of a Vulcanian eruption, except that in Peléan eruptions the volcano's structure is able to withstand more pressure, hence the eruption occurs as one large explosion rather than several smaller ones.

Volcanoes known to have Peléan activity include:

- Mount Pelée, Martinique. The 1902 eruption of Mount Pelée completely devastated the island, destroying the town of St. Pierre and leaving only 3 survivors. The eruption was directly preceded by lava dome growth.
- Mayon Volcano, the Philippines most active volcano. It has been the site of many different types of eruptions, Peléan included. Approximarly 40 ravines radiate from the summit and provide pathways for frequent pyroclastic flows and mudslides to the lowlands below. Mayon's most violent eruption occurred in 1814 and was responsible for over 1200 deaths.
- The 1951 Peléan eruption of Mount Lamington. Prior to this eruption the peak had not even been recognized as a volcano. Over 3,000 people were killed, and it has become a benchmark for studying large Peléan eruptions.

Plinian

Plinian eruptions (or Vesuvian) are a type of volcanic eruption, named for the historical AD 79 eruption of Mount Vesuvius that buried the Roman towns of Pompeii and Herculaneum, and specifically for its chronicler Pliny the Younger. The process powering Plinian eruptions starts in the magma chamber, where dissolved volatile gases are stored in the magma. The gases vesiculate and accumulate as they rise through the magma conduit. These bubbles agglutinate and once they reach a certain size (about 75% of the total volume of the magma conduit) they explode.

The narrow confines of the conduit force the gases and associated magma up, forming an eruptive column. Eruption velocity is controlled by the gas contents of the column, and low-strength surface rocks commonly crack under the pressure of the eruption, forming a flared outgoing structure that pushes the gases even faster.

These massive eruptive columns are the distinctive feature of a Plinian eruption, and reach up 2 to 45 kms (1 to 28 mi) into the atmosphere. The densest part of the plume, directly above the volcano, is driven internally by gas expansion. As it reaches higher into the air the plume expands and becomes less dense, convection and thermal expansion of volcanic ash drive it even further up into the stratosphere. At the top of the plume, powerful prevailing winds drive the plume in a direction away from the volcano.

These highly explosive eruptions are associated with volatile-rich dacitic to rhyolitic lavas, and occur most typically at stratovolcanoes. Eruptions can last anywhere from hours to days, with longer eruptions being associated with more felsic volcanoes. Although they are associated with felsic magma, Plinian eruptions can just as well occur at basaltic volcanoes, given that the magma chamber differentiates and has a structure rich in silicon dioxide.

Plinian eruptions are similar to both Vulcanian and Strombolian eruptions, except that rather than creating discrete explosive events, Plinian eruptions form sustained eruptive columns. They are also similar to Hawaiian lava fountains in that both eruptive types produce sustained eruption columns maintained by the growth of bubbles that move up at about the same speed as the magma surrounding them.

Regions affected by Plinian eruptions are subjected to heavy pumice airfall affecting an area 0.5 to 50 km^3 (0 to 12 cu mi) in size. The material in the ash plume eventually finds its way back to the ground, covering the landscape in a thick layer of many cubic kilometres of ash.

However the most dangerous eruptive feature are the pyroclastic flows generated by material collapse, which move down the side of the mountain at extreme speeds of up to 700 kms (435 mi) per hour and with the ability to extend the reach of the eruption hundreds of kilometres. The ejection of hot material from the volcano's summit melts snowbanks and ice deposits on the volcano, which mixes with tephra to form lahars, fast moving mudslides with the consistency of wet concrete that move at the speed of a river rapid.

Major Plinian eruptive events include:

- The historical AD 79 eruption of Mount Vesuvius buried the Roman towns of Pompeii and Herculaneum under a layer of ash and tephra. It is the model Plinian eruption. Mount Vesuvius has erupted multiple times since then, for example in 1822.
- The 1980 eruption of Mount St. Helens in Washington, which ripped apart the volcano's summit, was a Plinian eruption of Volcanic Explosivity Index (VEI) 5.
- The strongest types of erupions, with a VEI of 8, are so-called 'Ulta-Plinian' eruptions, such as the most recent one at Lake Toba 74 thousand years ago, which put out 2800 times the material erupted by Mount St. Helens in 1980.
- Hekla in Iceland, an example of basaltic Pilian volcanism being its 1947-48 eruption. The past 800 years have been a pattern of violent initial eruptions of pumice followed by prolonged extrusion of basaltic lava from the lower part of the volcano.
- Pinatubo in the Philippines on 15 June 1991, which produced 5 km^3 (1 cu mi) of dacitic magma, a 40 km (25 mi) high eruption column, and released 17 megatons of sulfur dioxide.

Phreatomagmatic Eruptions

Phreatomagmatic eruptions are eruptions that arise from interactions between water and magma. They are driven from thermal contraction (as opposed to magmatic eruptions, which are driven by thermal expansion) of magma when it comes in contact with water. This temperature difference between the two causes violent water-lava interactions that make up the eruption. The products of phreatomagmatic eruptions are believed to be more regular in shape and finer grained than the products of magmatic eruptions because of the differences in eruptive mechanisms.

There is debate about the exact nature of Phreatomagmatic eruptions, and some scientists believe that fuel-coolant reactions may be more critical to the explosive nature than thermal contraction. Fuel coolant reactions may fragment the volcanic material by propagating stress waves, widening cracks and increasing surface area that ultimetly lead to rapid cooling and explosive contraction-driven eruptions.

Surtseyan

A Surtseyan eruption (or hydrovolcanic) is a type of volcanic eruption caused by shallow-water interactions between water and lava, named so after its most famous example, the eruption and formation of the island of Surtsey off the coast of Iceland in 1963. Surtseyan eruptions are the 'wet' equivalent of ground-based Strombolian eruptions, but because of where they are taking place they are much more explosive. This is because as water is heated by lava, it flashes in steam and expands violently, fragmenting the magma it is in contact with into fine-grained ash. Surtseyan eruptions are the hallmark of shallow-water volcanic oceanic islands, however they are not specifically confined to them. Surtseyan eruptions can happen on land as well, and are caused by rising magma that comes into contact with an aquifer (water-bearing rock formation) at shallow levels under the volcano. The products of Surtseyan eruptions are generally oxidized palagonite basalts (though andesitic eruptions do occur, albeit rarely), and like Strombolian eruptions Surtseyan eruptions are generally continuous or otherwise rhythmic.

A distinct defining feature of a Surtseyan eruption is the formation of a pyroclastic surge (or *base surge*), a ground hugging radial cloud that develops along with the eruption column. Base surges are caused by the gravitational collapse of a vaperous eruptive column, one that is denser overall then a regular volcanic column. The densest part of the cloud is nearest to the vent, resulting a wedge shape. Associated with these laterally moving rings are dune-shaped depositions of rock left behind by the lateral movement. These are occasionally disrupted by bomb sags, rock that was flung out by the explosive eruption and followed a ballistic path to the ground. Accumulations of wet, spherical ash known as accretionary lapilli is another common surge indicator.

Over time Surtseyan eruptions tend to form maars, broad low-relief volcanic craters dug into the ground, and tuff rings, circular structures built of rapidly quenched lava. These structures are associated with a single vent eruption, however if eruptions arise along fracture zones a rift zone may be dug out; these eruptions tend to be more violent then the ones forming a tuff ring or maars, an example being the 1886 eruption of Mount Tarawera. Littoral cones are another hydrovolcanic feature, generated by the explosive deposition of basaltic tephra (although they are not truly volcanic vents). They form when lava accumulates within cracks in lava, superheats and explodes in a steam explosion, breaking the rock apart and depositing it on the volcano's flank. Consecutive explosions of this type eventually generate the cone.

Volcanoes known to have Surtseyan activity include:

- Surtsey, Iceland. The volcano built itself up from depth and emerged above the Atlantic Ocean off the coast of Iceland in 1963. Initial hydrovolcanics were highly explosive, but as the volcano grew out rising lava started to interact less with the water and more with the air, until finally Surtseyan activity waned and became more Strombolian in character.

- Ukinrek Maars in Alaska, 1977, and Capelinhos in the Azores, 1957, both examples of above-water Surtseyan activity.
- Mount Tarawera in New Zealand erupted along a rift zone in 1886, killing 150 people.
- Ferdinandea, a seamount in the Mediterranean Sea, breached sea level in July 1831 and was the source of a dispute over sovereignty between Italy, France, and Great Britain. The volcano did not build tuff cones strongly enough to withstand erosion, and disappeared back below the waves soon after it appeared.
- The underwater volcano Hunga Tonga in Tonga breached sea level in 2009. Both of its vents exhibited Surtseyan activity for much of the time. It was also the site of an earlier eruption in May 1988.

Submarine

Submarine eruptions are a type of volcanic eruption that occurs underwater. An estimated 75 per cent of the total volcanic eruptive volume is generated by submarine eruptions near mid ocean ridges alone, however because of the problems associated with detecting deep sea volcanics, they remained virtually unknown until advances in the 1990s made it possible to observe them.

Submarine eruptions are generated by seamounts (underwater volcanoes), and are driven by one of two processes. Volcanoes near plate boundaries and mid-ocean ridges are built by the decompression melting of mantle rock that floats up to the crustal surface. Eruptions near subducting zones, meanwhile, are driven by subducting plates that adds volatiles to the rising plate, raising its melting point. Each process generates different rock; mid-ocean ridge volcanics are primarily basaltic, whereas subduction flows are mostly calc-alkaline, and more explosive and viscous.

Spreading rates along mid-ocean ridges vary widely, from 2 cm (0.8 in) per year at the Mid-Atlantic Ridge, to up to 16 cm (6 in) along the East Pacific Rise. Higher spreading rates are a probably cause for higher levels of volcanism. The technology for studying seamount eruptions did not exist until advancements in hydrophone technology made it possible to 'listen' to acoustic waves, known as T-waves, released by submarine earthquakes associated with submarine volcanic eruptions. The reason for this is that land-based seismometers cannot detect sea-based earthquakes below a magnitude of 4, but acoustic waves travel well in water and long periods of time. A system in the North Pacific, maintained by the United States Navy and originally intended for the detection of submarines, has detected an event on average every 2 to 3 years.

The most common underwater flow is pillow lava, a circular lava flow named after its unusual shape. Less common are glassy, marginal sheet flows, indicative of larger-scale flows. Volcaniclastic sedimentary rocks are common in shallow-water environments. As plate movement starts to carry the volcanoes away from their eruptive source, eruption rates start to die down, and water erosion grinds the volcano down. The final stages of eruption caps the seamount in alkalic flows. There are about 100,000 deepwater volcanoes in the world, although most are beyond the active stage of their life. Some exemplery seamounts are Loihi Seamount, Bowie Seamount, Cross Seamount, and Denson Seamount.

Subglacial

Subglacial eruptions are a type of volcanic eruption characterized by interactions between lava and ice, often under a glacier. The nature of glaciovolcanism dictates that it occurs at areas of high latitude and high altitude. It has been suggested that subglacial volcanoes that are not actively erupting often dump heat into the ice covering them, producing meltwater. This meltwater mix means that subglacial eruptions often generate dangerous jökulhlaups (floods) and lahars.

The study of glaciovolcanism is still a relatively new field. Early accounts described the unusual flat-topped steep-sided volcanoes (called tuyas) in Iceland that were suggested to have formed from eruptions below ice. The first English-language paper on the subject was published in 1947 by William Henry Mathews, describing the Tuya Butte field in northwest British Columbia. The eruptive process that builds these structures, originally inferred in the paper, begins with volcanic growth below the glacier. At first the eruptions resemble those that occur in the deep sea, forming piles of pillow lava at the base of the volcanic structure. Some of the lava shatters when it comes in contact with the cold ice, forming a glassy breccia called hyaloclastite. After a while the ice finally melts into a lake, and the more explosive eruptions of Surtseyan activity begins, building up flanks made up of mostly hyaloclastite. Eventually the lake boils off from continued volcanism, and the lava flows become more effusive and thicken as the lava cools much more slowly, often forming columnar jointing. Well-preserved tuyas show all of these stages, for example Hjorleifshofdi in Iceland.

Products of volcano-ice interactions stand as various structures, whose shape is dependent on complex eruptive and environmental interactions. Glacial volcanism is a good indicator of past ice distribution, making it an important climatic marker. Since they are imbedded in ice, as ice retracts worldwide there are concerns that tuyas and other structures may destabalize, resulting in mass landslides. Evidence of volcanic-glacial interactions are evident in Iceland and parts of British Columbia, and it's even possible that they play a role in deglaciation.

Glaciovolcanic products have been identified in Iceland, British Columbia, Hawaii and Alaska, the Cascade Range, South America and even on the planet Mars. Volcanoes known to have subglacial activity include:

- Mauna Kea in tropical Hawaii. There is evidence of past subglacial eruptive activity on the volcano in the form of a subglacial deposit on its summit. The eruptions originated about 10,000 years ago, during the last ice age, when the summit of Mauna Kea was covered in ice.
- In 2008, the British Antarctic Survey reported a volcanic eruption under the Antarctica ice sheet 2,200 years ago. It is believed to be that this was the biggest eruption in Antarctica in the last 10,000 years. Volcanic ash deposits from the volcano were identified through an airborne radar survey, buried under later snowfalls in the Hudson Mountains, close to Pine Island Glacier.
- Iceland, well known for both glaciers and volcanoes, is often a site of subglacial eruptions. An example an eruption under the Vatnajökull ice cap in 1996, which occurred under an estimated 2,500 ft (762 m) of ice.
- As part of the search for life on Mars, scientists have suggested that there may be subglacial volcanoes on the red planet. Several potential sites of such volcanism have been reviewed, and compared extensively with similar features in Iceland:

> "Viable microbial communities have been found living in deep (2800 m) geothermal groundwater at 349 K and pressures over 300 bar..Furthermore, microbes have been postulated to exist in basaltic rocks in rinds of altered volcanic glass. All of these conditions could exist in polar regions of Mars today where subglacial volcanism has occurred".
>
> —*Jack Farmer, Arizona State University*

Phreatic Eruptions

Phreatic eruptions (or steam-blast eruptions) are a type of eruption driven by the expansion of steam. When cold ground or surface water coming into contact with hot rock or magma it superheats and explodes, fracturing the surrounding rock and thrusting out a mixture of steam, water, ash, volcanic bombs, and volcanic blocks. The distinguishing feature of phreatic explosions is that they only blast out fragments of pre-existing solid rock from the volcanic conduit; no new magma is erupted. Because they are driven by the cracking of rock stata under pressure, Phreatic activity does not always result in an eruption; if the rock face is strong enough to withstand the explosive force, outright eruptions may not occur, although cracks in the rock will probably develop and weaken it, furthering future eruptions.

Often a precursor of future volcanic activity, Phreatic eruptions are generally weak, although there have been exceptions. Some Phreatic events may be triggered by earthquake activity, another volcanic precursor, and they may also travel along dike lines. Phreatic eruptions form base surges, lahars, avalanches, and volcanic block 'rain'. They may also release deadly toxic gas able to sufficate anyone in range of the eruption.

3 Volcanic Ash

Volcanic ash consists of small tephra, which are bits of pulverized rock and glass created by volcanic eruptions, less than 2 millimetres (0.1 in) in diametre. There are three mechanisms of volcanic ash formation: gas release under decompression causing magmatic eruptions; thermal contraction from chilling on contact with water causing phreatomagmatic eruptions, and ejection of entrained particles during steam eruptions causing phreatic eruptions. The violent nature of volcanic eruptions involving steam results in the magma and solid rock surrounding the vent being torn into particles of clay to sand size. Volcanic ash can lead to breathing problems and malfunctions in machinery, and clouds of it can threaten aircraft and alter weather patterns.

Ash deposited on the ground after an eruption is known as ashfall deposit. Significant accumulations of ashfall can lead to the immediate destruction of most of the local ecosystem, as well the collapse of roofs on man-made structures. Over time, ashfall can lead to the creation of fertile soils. Ashfall can also become cemented together to form a solid rock called tuff. Over geologic time, the ejection of large quantities of ash can produce an ash cone.

There are three mechanisms of volcanic ash formation:

1. Gas release under decompression causing magmatic eruptions;
2. Thermal contraction from chilling on contact with water causing phreatomagmatic eruptions;
3. Ejection of entrained particles during steam eruptions causing phreatic eruptions. The violent nature of volcanic eruptions involving steam results in the magma and solid rock surrounding the vent being torn into particles of clay to sand size.

If a volcanic eruption occurs beneath glacial ice, cold water from melted ice chills the lava quickly and fragments it into glass, creating small glass particles that get carried into the eruption plume. This can create a glass-rich plume in the upper atmosphere which is particularly hazardous to aircraft.

The plume that is often seen above an erupting volcano is composed primarily of ash and steam. The very fine particles may be carried for many miles, settling out as a dust-like layer across the landscape. This is known as an ashfall. If liquid magma is ejected as a spray, the particles will solidify in the air as small fragments of volcanic glass. Unlike the ash that forms from burning wood or other combustible materials, volcanic ash is hard and abrasive. It does not dissolve in water, and it conducts electricity, especially when it is wet.

Ashfall can become cemented together by heat to form a solid rock called tuff. Ashfall breaks down over time, forming highly fertile soil, which has made many volcanic regions densely cultivated and inhabited despite the inherent dangers.

In 1783, the Laki eruption killed about one-fifth of Iceland's population, and sent a huge toxic cloud of ash and sulphurous gases across Western Europe. In Britain alone, it has been estimated that 23,000 died from the poisoning.

Atmospheric Effects

When ash begins to fall during daylight hours, the sky turns hazy and a pale yellow colour. The ashfall may become so dense that daylight turns the sky gray to pitch black, with the ash severely restricting visibility and deadening sound. A darkened ash sky lowers temperatures during daylight hours from what would otherwise be expected. Loud thunder, lightning, as well as the strong smell of sulfur accompany an ashfall. If rain accompanies an ashfall, the tiny particles turn into a slurry of slippery mud. Rain and lightning combined with ash can lead to power outages, breakdowns of communication, and disorientation.

Volcanic ash particles have a maximum residence time in the troposphere of a few weeks. The finest tephra particles remain in the stratosphere for only a few months, they have only minor climatic effects, and they can be spread around the world by high-altitude winds. This suspended material contributes to spectacular sunsets. The major climate influence from volcanic eruptions is caused by gaseous sulfur compounds, chiefly sulfur dioxide, which reacts with OH and water in the stratosphere to create sulfate aerosols with a residence time of about 2-3 years.

The most devastating effect of volcanic ash comes from pyroclastic flows. These occur when a volcanic eruption creates an 'avalanche' of hot ash, gases, and rocks that flow at high speed down the flanks of the volcano. These flows can be impossible to outrun. They can also be difficult to predict. In many cases prediction is based on the topography of a region, but a valley may fill and overflow. In 1902, the city of St. Pierre in Martinique was destroyed by a pyroclastic flow which killed over 29,000 people.

Fluorine poisoning and death can occur in livestock that graze on ash-covered grass if fluoride is present in high concentrations. Inhaling volcanic ash may cause problems for people whose respiratory system is already compromised by disorders such as asthma or emphysema. The abrasive texture can cause irritation and scratching of the surface of the eyes. People who wear contact lenses should wear glasses during an ashfall, to prevent eye damage. Furthermore, the combination of volcanic ash with moisture in the lungs can create a substance akin to liquid cement.

Therefore, people should take caution to filter the air they breathe with a damp cloth or a face mask when facing an ashfall. Ash is very dense, as only 100 millimetres (3.9 in) of ash leads to the collapse of weaker roofs. A fall of 300 millimetres (12 in) leads to the death of most vegetation, livestock, the wiping out of aquatic life in nearby lakes and rivers, and unusable roads. Accompanied by rain and lightning, ashfall leads to power outages, prevents communication, and disorients people.

Aviation

According to Dr. Dougal Jerram, an earth scientist at the Centre for Research into Earth Energy Systems, University of Durham, UK, "Eruptions which are charged with gas start to froth and expand as they reach the surface. This results in explosive eruptions and this fine ash being sent up into the atmosphere. If it is ejected high enough, the ash can reach the high winds and be dispersed around the globe, for example, from Iceland to Europe. These high winds are exactly where the aeroplanes cruise." Volcanic ash can harm a plane mainly in four ways:

1. Sandblasting Effect

Ash can 'blind' pilots by sandblasting the windscreen requiring an instrument landing, damage the fuselage, and coat the plane (KLM Flight 867 and BA Flight 9). In addition, the sandblasting effect can damage the landing lights, making their beams diffuse and unable to be projected in the forward direction (BA Flight 9). Propellor aircraft are also endangered.

2. Clogging of the Plane's Sensors

Accumulation of ash can also block an aircraft's pitot tubes. This can lead to failure of the aircraft's air speed indicators.

3. Electromagnetic Wave Insulation

Volcanic ash particles are charged and disturb communication by radio.

4. Combustion Power Failure

Volcanic ash damages machinery. The effect on jet aircraft engines is particularly severe as large amounts of air are sucked in during combustion operation, posing a great danger to aircraft flying near ash clouds. Very fine volcanic ash particles (particularly glass-rich if from an eruption under ice) sucked into a jet engine melt at about 1,100° C, fusing onto the blades and other parts of the turbine (which operates at about 1,400° C).

The effect on the operation of a jet engine is often to cause it to cut out–failure of all a plane's engines is common:

- Volcanic ash particles can erode and destroy parts, drive it out-of-balance, and cause jams in rotating machinery.
- Also simple lack of oxygen is given as a probable cause of engine failure (fooling of the air/fuel control).
- Fooling of the engine temperature sensors (KLM Flight 867).
- And compressor stall and flameout can be other reason.

The standard emergency procedure when jet engines begin to fail had been to increase power, which makes the problem worse. The best procedure is to throttle back the engines, turn on engine and wing anti-ice devices (it helps to avoid compressor and wing stall), and to lose height so as to drop below the ash cloud as quickly as possible. The inrush of cold, clean air is usually enough to cool, solidify, and shatter the glass, unclogging the engines.

Occurrences

There are many instances of damage to jet aircraft as a result of an ash encounter. After the Galunggung, Indonesia volcanic event in 1982, a British Airways Flight 9 flew through an ash cloud; all four engines cut out. The plane descended from 36,000 feet (11,000 m) to 12,000 feet (3,700 m), where the engines could be restarted. On December 15, 1989 a KLM Boeing 747-400 (Flight 867) flying from Amsterdam Schiphol Airport to Anchorage International Airport encountered similar problems near Mount Redoubt (Alaska). The damage was 80 million US$; there was 80 kg ash in each turbine; it took 3 months work to repair the plane.

In April 2010, airspace all over Europe was closed–which was unprecedented–due to the presence of volcanic ash in the upper atmosphere from the eruption of the Icelandic volcano Eyjafjallajökull. On 15 April 2010 the Finnish Air Force halted training flights when damage was found from volcanic dust ingestion by the engines of one of its Boeing F-18 Hornet fighters. On 22 April 2010 UK RAF Typhoon training flights were also temporarily suspended after deposits of volcanic ash were found in a jet's engines.

A distinction can be made between flight through (or in the immediate vicinity of) an eruption plume, and flight through the so-called affected airspace. Volcanic ash in the immediate vicinity of the eruption plume is of an entirely different particle size range and density to that found in downwind dispersal clouds, which contain only the finest grade of ash. The actual level of ash loading which catastrophically affects normal engine operation has not yet been established, beyond the knowledge that relatively high ash densities must exist for this to happen. Whether this silica-melt risk still remains at the much lower ash densities characteristic of downstream ash clouds is currently unclear. This is however a serious safety hazard which requires preventive risk-management strategies, in line with other comparable aviation hazards.

Detection and Avoidance

In June 2010, Easyjet airline company has unveiled a system that it says will allow airlines to safely fly around ash clouds. The system is based on 20-year old research by Fred Prata at the Australian research organisation CSIRO and now based at the Norwegian Institute for Air Research.

Marine Transportation

Similar to aviation, volcanic ash has detrimental effects on marine transportation machinery. However, it poses much less of a hazard—an aircraft encountering an ash plume has engines sucking in huge amounts of air, and cannot stop them until the plume passes, possibly days later.

Advisories Concerning Ongoing Events

Increasing numbers of airplane incidents from atmospheric ash prompted a 1991 aviation industry meeting to decide how best to distribute information about ash events. One solution was the creation of Volcanic Ash Advisory Centers. There is one VAAC for each of nine regions of the world. VAACs can issue advisories and serve as liaisons between meteorologists, volcanologists, and the aviation industry.

4 Magma

Magma (from Greek μ μa 'paste') is a mixture of molten rock, volatiles and solids that is found beneath the surface of the Earth, and may also exist on other terrestrial planets. Besides molten rock, magma may also contain suspended crystals and gas bubbles. Magma often collects in magma chambers that may feed a volcano or turn into a pluton. Magma is capable of intrusion into adjacent rocks, extrusion onto the surface as lava, and explosive ejection as tephra to form pyroclastic rock.

Magma is a complex high-temperature fluid substance. Temperatures of most magmas are in the range 700° C to 1300° C (or 1300° F to 2400° F), but very rare carbonatite melts may be as cool as 600° C, and komatiite melts may have been as hot as 1600° C. Most are silicate mixtures.

Environments of magma formation and compositions are commonly correlated. Environments include subduction zones, continental rift zones, mid-oceanic ridges, and hotspots, some of which are interpreted as mantle plumes. Despite being found in such widespread locales, the bulk of the Earth's crust and mantle is not molten. Rather, most of the Earth takes the form of a rheid, a form of solid that can move or deform under pressure. Magma, as liquid, preferentially forms in high temperature, low pressure environments within several kilometres of the Earth's surface.

Magma compositions may evolve after formation by fractional crystallization, contamination, and magma mixing. By definition, all igneous rock is formed from magma.

While the study of magma has historically relied on observing magma in the form of lava outflows, magma has been encountered *in situ* three times during drilling projects—twice in Iceland, and once in Hawaii.

Partial Melting

Melting of solid rock to form magma is controlled by three physical parameters: its temperature, pressure, and composition. Mechanisms are discussed in the entry for igneous rock.

When rocks melt they do so incrementally and gradually; most rocks are made of several minerals, all of which have different melting points, and the physical/chemical relationships controlling melting are complex. As a rock melts, its volume changes. When enough rock is melted, the small globules of melt (generally occurring in between mineral grains) link up and soften the rock. Under pressure within the earth, as little as a fraction of a percent partial melting may be sufficient to cause melt to be squeezed from its source.

Melts can stay in place long enough to melt to 20 per cent or even 35 per cent, but rocks are rarely melted in excess of 50 per cent, because eventually the melted rock mass becomes a crystal and melt mush that can then ascend *en masse* as a diapir, which may then cause further decompression melting.

Geochemical Implications of Partial Melting

The degree of partial melting is critical for determining what type of magma is produced. The degree of partial melting required to form a melt can be estimated by considering the relative enrichment of incompatible elements versus compatible elements. Incompatible elements commonly include potassium, barium, caesium, rubidium.

Rock types produced by small degrees of partial melting in the Earth's mantle are typically alkaline (Ca, Na), potassic (K) and/or peralkaline (high aluminium to silica ratio). Typically, primitive melts of this composition form lamprophyre, lamproite, kimberlite and sometimes nepheline-bearing mafic rocks such as alkali basalts and essexite gabbros or even carbonatite.

Pegmatite may be produced by low degrees of partial melting of the crust. Some granite-composition magmas are eutectic (or cotectic) melts, and they may be produced by low to high degrees of partial melting of the crust, as well as by fractional crystallization. At high degrees of partial melting of the crust, granitoids such as tonalite, granodiorite and monzonite can be produced, but other mechanisms are typically important in producing them.

Primary Melts

When a rock melts, the liquid as a *primary melt.* Primary melts have not undergone any differentiation and represent the starting composition of a magma. In nature it is rare to find primary melts. The leucosomes of migmatites are examples of primary melts. Primary melts derived from the mantle are especially important, and are known as *primitive melts* or primitive magmas. By finding the primitive magma composition of a magma series it is possible to model the composition of the mantle from which a melt was formed, which is important in understanding evolution of the mantle.

Parental Melts

Where it is impossible to find the primitive or primary magma composition, it is often useful to attempt to identify a parental melt. A parental melt is a magma composition from which the observed range of magma chemistries has been derived by the processes of igneous differentiation. It need not be a primitive melt.

For instance, a series of basalt flows are assumed to be related to one another. A composition from which they could reasonably be produced by fractional crystallization is termed a *parental melt.* Fractional crystallization models would be produced to test the hypothesis that they share a common parental melt.

At high degrees of partial melting of the mantle, komatiite and picrite are produced.

Migration

Magma develops within the mantle or crust when the temperature-pressure conditions favor the molten state. Magma rises toward the Earth's surface when it is less dense than the surrounding rock and when a structural zone allows movement. Magma develops or collects in areas called magma chambers. Magma can remain in a chamber until it cools and crystallizes forming igneous rock, it erupts as a volcano, or moves into another magma chamber.

There are two known processes by which magma ceases to exist, by volcanic eruption or by crystallization within the crust or mantle to form a pluton. In both cases the bulk of the magma eventually cools and forms igneous rocks.

When magma cools it begins to form solid mineral phases, some of them settles at the bottom of the magma chamber forming cumulates that might form mafic layered intrusions. Magma that cools slowly within a magma chamber usually ends up as forming bodies of plutonic rocks such as gabbro, diorite and granite depending on the composition of the magma, while if the magma is erupted it forms volcanic rocks such as basalt, andesite and rhyolite (the extrusive equivalents of gabbro, diorite and granite respectively).

Volcanism

During a volcanic eruption the magma that leaves the underground is called lava. Lava cools and solidifies relatively quickly compared to underground bodies of magma. This fast cooling does not allow crystals to grow large, and a part of the melt does not crystallize at all, becoming glass (obsidian).

Before and during volcanic eruptions, volatiles such as CO_2 and H_2O partially leave the melt through a process known as exsolution. Magma with low water content becomes increasingly viscous. If massive exsolution occurs when magma heads upwards during a volcanic eruption, the resulting eruption is usually explosive.

Composition, Melt Structure and Properties

Silicate melts are composed mainly of silicon, oxygen, aluminium, alkalis (sodium, potassium, calcium), magnesium and iron. Silicon atoms are in tetrahedral coordination with oxygen, as in almost all silicate minerals, but in melts atomic order is preserved only over short distances. The physical behaviours of melts depend upon their atomic structures as well as upon temperature and pressure and composition.

Viscosity is a key melt property in understanding the behaviour of magmas. More silica-rich melts are typically more polymerized, with more linkage of silica tetrahedra, and so are more viscous. Dissolution of water drastically reduces melt viscosity. Higher-temperature melts are less viscous.

Generally speaking, more mafic magmas, such as those that form basalt, are hotter and less viscous than more silica-rich magmas, such as those that form rhyolite. Low viscosity leads to gentler, less explosive eruptions.

Main Article: Igneous Differentiation

Characteristics of several different magma types are as follows:

- Ultramafic (Picritic)
- SiO_2 < 45 per cent
- Fe-Mg >8 per cent up to 32 per cent MgO
- Temperature: up to 1500° C
- Viscosity: Very Low
- Eruptive behaviour: gentle or very explosive (kimberilites)
- Distribution: divergent plate boundaries, hot spots, convergent plate boundaries; komatiite and other ultramafic lavas are mostly Archean and were formed from a higher geothermal gradient and are unknown in the present.
- Mafic (basaltic).
- SiO_2 < 50 per cent
- FeO and MgO typically < 10 wt per cent
- Temperature: up to ~1300° C
- Viscosity: Low
- Eruptive behaviour: gentle
- Distribution: divergent plate boundaries, hot spots, convergent plate boundaries
- Intermediate (andesitic)
- SiO_2 ~ 60 per cent
- Fe-Mg: ~ 3 per cent
- Temperature: ~1000° C
- Viscosity: Intermediate
- Eruptive behaviour: explosive or effusive
- Distribution: convergent plate boundaries, island arcs
- Felsic (rhyolitic)

- SiO_2 >70 per cent
- Fe-Mg: ~ 2 per cent
- Temp: < 900° C
- Viscosity: High
- Eruptive behaviour: explosive or effusive
- Distribution: hot spots in continental crust (Yellowstone National Park), continental rifts

Temperature

At any given pressure and for any given composition of rock, a rise in temperature past the solidus will cause melting. Within the solid earth, the temperature of a rock is controlled by the geothermal gradient and the radioactive decay within the rock. The geothermal gradient averages about 25° C/km with a wide range from a low of 5-10° C/km within oceanic trenches and subduction zones to 30-80° C/km under mid-ocean ridges and volcanic arc environments.

Pressure

As magma buoyantly rises it will cross the solidus-liquidus and its temperature will reduce by adiabatic cooling. At this point it will liquefy and if erupted onto the surface will form lava. Melting can also occur due to a reduction in pressure by a process known as decompression melting.

Composition

It is usually very difficult to change the bulk composition of a large mass of rock, so composition is the basic control on whether a rock will melt at any given temperature and pressure. The composition of a rock may also be considered to include *volatile* phases such as water and carbon dioxide.

The presence of volatile phases in a rock under pressure can stabilize a melt fraction. The presence of even

0.8 per cent water may reduce the temperature of melting by as much as 100° C. Conversely, the loss of water and volatiles from a magma may cause it to essentially freeze or solidify.

Also a major portion of all magma is silica, which is a compound of silicon and oxygen. Magma also contains gases, which expand as the magma rises. Magma that is high in silica resists flowing, so expanding gases are trapped in it. Pressure builds up until the gases blast out in a violent, dangerous explosion. Magma that is relatively poor in silica flows easily, so gas bubbles move up through it and escape fairly gently.

Phreatomagmatic Eruption

Phreatomagmatic eruptions are defined as juvenile forming eruptions as a result of interaction between water and magma. They are different from magmatic and phreatic eruptions. The products of phreatomagmatic eruptions contain juvenile clasts, unlike phreatic eruptions and are the result of interaction between magma and water unlike magmatic eruptions. It is very common for a large explosive eruption to have magmatic and phreatomagmatic components.

Several competing theories exist as to the exact mechanism of ash formation. The most common is the theory of explosive thermal contraction of particles under rapid cooling from contact with water. In many cases the water is supplied by the sea, for example Surtsey. In other cases the water may be present in a lake or Caldera-lake, for example Santorini where the phreatomagmatic component of the Minoan eruption was a result of both a lake and later the sea. There have also been examples of interaction between magma and water in an aquifer, many of the cinder cones on Tenerife are believed to be phreatomagmatic because of these circumstances.

The other competing theory is based on fuel-coolant reactions, which have been modeled for the nuclear industry. Under this theory the magma (in this case the fuel) fragments upon contact with a coolant (the sea, a lake or aquifer), the propagating stress waves and thermal contraction widening cracks and increasing the interaction surface area leading to explosively rapid cooling rates. The two mechanisms proposed are very similar and the reality is most likely a combination of both.

Deposits

Phreatomagmatic ash is formed by the same mechanisms across a wide range of compositions, basic and acidic. Blocky and equant clasts with low vesicularities are formed. The deposits of phreatomagmatic explosive eruptions are also believed to be better sorted and finer grained than the deposits of magmatic eruption. This is a result of the much higher fragmentation of phreatomagmatic eruptions.

Hyaloclastite

This is the term used to describe glass found with pillow basalts that were produced by non-explosive quenching and fracturing of basaltic glass. These are still classed as phreatomagmatic eruptions as they produce juvenile clasts from the interaction of water and magma. They can be formed at water depths of >500 m, where hydrostatic pressure is high enough to inhibit vesiculation in basaltic magma.

Hyalotuff

Hyalotuff is the term used to define rocks formed by the explosive fragmentation of glass during phreatomagmatic eruptions at shallow water depths (or within aquifers). Hyalotuffs have a layered nature that is believed to be a result of dampened oscillation in discharge rate with a period of several minutes. The deposits are much finer grained than the deposits of magmatic eruptions, due to the much higher fragmentation of the type of eruption. The deposits appear better sorted than magmatic deposits in the field because of their fine nature, but when grain size analysis is undertaken the deposits are much more poorly sorted than their magmatic counterparts. A clast known as an accretionary lapilli is distinctive to phreatomagmatic deposits, and is a major factor for identification in the field. Accretionary lapilli form as a result of the cohesive properties of wet ash, causing the particles to bind. They have a circular structure when viewed in hand specimen and under the microscope.

A further control on the morphology and characteristics of a deposit is the water to magma ratio. It is believed that the products of phreatomagmatic eruptions are fine grained and poorly sorted where the magma/water ratio is high but when there is a lower magma/water ratio the deposits may be coarser and better sorted.

Surface Features

There are two types of vent landforms from the explosive interaction of magma and ground or surface water; *Tuff Cones* and *Tuff Rings.* Both of the landforms are associated with monogenetic volcanoes and polygenetic volcanoes. In the case of polygenetic volcanoes they are often interbedded with lavas, ignimbrites and ash- and lapilli-fall deposits.

Minoan Eruption of Santorini

Santorini is part of the Southern Aegean volcanic arc, 140 km north of Crete. The Minoan eruption of Santorini, was the latest eruption and occurred in the first half of the 17th century B.C. The eruption was of predominantly rhyodacite composition. The Minoan eruption had four phases. Phase 1 was a white to pink pumice fallout with dispersal axis trending ESE. The deposit has a maximum thickness of 6 m and ash flow layers are interbedded at the top. Phase 2 has ash and lapilli beds that are cross stratified with mega-ripples and dune like structures. The deposit thicknesses vary from 10 cm to 12 m. Phases 3 and 4 are pyroclastic density current deposits. Phases 1 and 3 were phreatomagmatic.

Pinatubo, 1991

Mount Pinatubo is on the Central Luzon landmass between the South China Sea and the Philippine Sea. The 1991 eruption of Pinatubo was andesite and dacite in the pre-climactic phase but only dacite in the climactic phase. The climactic phase had a volume of 3.7-5.3 km^3. The eruption consisted of sequentially increasing ash emissions, dome growth, 4 vertical eruptions with continued dome growth, 13 pyroclastic flows and a climactic vertical eruption with associated pyroclastic flows. The pre-climactic phase was phreatomagmatic.

Lake Taupo

The Hatepe eruption in 180 AD was the latest major eruption at Lake Taupo in New Zealand's Taupo Volcanic Zone. There was minor initial phreatomagmatic activity followed by the dry venting of 6 km^3 of rhyolite forming the Hatepe Plinian Pumice. The vent was then infiltrated by large amounts of water causing the phreatomagmatic eruption that deposited the 2.5 km^3 Hatepe Ash. The water eventually stopped the eruption though large amounts of water were still erupted from the vent. The eruption resumed with phreatomagmatic activity that deposited the Rotongaio Ash.

Magma Chamber

A magma chamber is a large underground pool of molten rock found beneath the surface of the Earth. The molten rock in such a chamber is under great pressure, and given enough time, that pressure can gradually fracture the rock around it creating outlets for the magma. If it finds a way to the surface, then the result will be a volcanic eruption; consequently many volcanoes are situated over magma chambers.

Magma chambers are hard to detect, and most of the known ones are therefore close to the surface of the Earth, commonly between 1 km and 10 km under the surface. In geological terms this is extremely close to the surface, although in human terms it is considerably deep underground.

Dynamics of Magma Chambers

Magma rises through fractures from beneath the crust because it is less dense than the surrounding rock. When the magma cannot find a path upwards it pools into a magma chamber. As more magma rises up below it, the pressure in the chamber grows.

If magma resides in a chamber for a long period, then it can become stratified with lower density components rising to the top and denser materials sinking. It can also start to cool, with the higher melting point components such as olivine crystallising out of the solution, particularly near to the cooler walls of the chamber, and forming a denser conglomerate of minerals which sinks. Any subsequent eruption may produce distinctly layered deposits, for example the deposits from the 79 AD eruption of Mount Vesuvius include a thick layer of white pumice from the upper portion of the magma chamber overlayed with a similar layer of grey pumice produced from material erupted later from lower down in the chamber.

Another effect of the cooling of the chamber is that the solidifying crystals will release the gas (primarily steam) previously dissolved when they were liquid, causing the pressure in the chamber to rise, possibly sufficiently to produce an eruption. Additionally, the removal of the lower melting point components will tend to make the magma more viscous (by increasing the concentration of silicates). Thus, stratification of a magma chamber may result in an increase in the amount of gas within the magma near the top of the chamber, and also make this magma more viscous; potentially leading to a more explosive eruption than would be the case had the chamber not become stratified.

If the magma is not vented to the surface in a volcanic eruption it will slowly cool and crystallize at depth to form an intrusive igneous body composed of granite or gabbro.

Often, a volcano may have a deep magma chamber many kilometres down, which supplies a shallower chamber near the summit. The location of magma chambers can be mapped using seismology: seismic waves from earthquakes move more slowly through liquid rock than solid, allowing measurements to pinpoint the regions of slow movement which identify magma chambers.

As a volcano erupts, emptying the magma chamber, the surrounding rock will collapse into it. If a large amount of magma is erupted, causing the chamber to reduce considerably in volume, then this can result in a depression at the surface called a caldera.

5 Lava

Lava is molten rock expelled by a volcano during an eruption. This molten rock is formed in the interior of some planets, including Earth, and some of their satellites. When first erupted from a volcanic vent, lava is a liquid at temperatures from 700° C to 1,200° C (1,300° F to 2,200° F). Up to 100,000 times as viscous as water, lava can flow great distances before cooling and solidifying because of its thixotropic and shear thinning properties.

A *lava flow* is a moving outpouring of lava, which is created during a non-explosive effusive eruption. When it has stopped moving, lava solidifies to form igneous rock. The term *lava flow* is commonly shortened to *lava.* Explosive eruptions produce a mixture of volcanic ash and other fragments called tephra, rather than lava flows. The word 'lava' comes from Italian, and is probably derived from the Latin word *labes* which means a fall or slide. The first use in connection with extruded magma (molten rock below the Earth's surface) was apparently in a short account written by Francesco Serao on the eruption of Vesuvius between May 14 and June 4, 1737. Serao described 'a flow of fiery lava' as an analogy to the flow of water and mud down the flanks of the volcano following heavy rain.

In general, the composition of a lava determines its behaviour more than the temperature of its eruption.

Composition

Igneous rocks, which form lava flows when erupted, can be classified into three chemical types; *felsic*, *intermediate*, and *mafic* (four if one includes the super-heated *ultramafic*). These classes are primarily chemical; however, the chemistry of lava also tends to correlate with the magma temperature, its viscosity and its mode of eruption.

Felsic Lava

Felsic (or silicic) lavas such as rhyolite and dacite typically form lava spines, lava domes or 'coulees' (which are thick, short lavas) and are associated with pyroclastic (fragmental) deposits. Most Silicic lava flows are extremely viscous, and typically fragment as they extrude, producing blocky autobreccias. The high viscosity and strength are the result of their chemistry, which is high in silica, aluminium, potassium, sodium, and calcium, forming a polymerized liquid rich in feldspar and quartz, which thus has a higher viscosity than other magma types. Felsic magmas can erupt at temperatures as low as 650 to 750° C. Unusually hot (>950° C) rhyolite lavas, however, may flow for distances of many tens of kilometres, such as in the Snake River Plain of the northwestern United States.

Intermediate Lava

Intermediate or andesitic lavas are lower in aluminium and silica, and usually somewhat richer in magnesium and iron. Intermediate lavas form andesite domes and block lavas, and may occur on steep composite volcanoes, such as in the Andes. Poorer in aluminium and silica than felsic lavas, and also commonly hotter (in the range of 750 to 950° C), they tend to be less viscous. Greater temperatures tend to destroy polymerized bonds within the magma, promoting more fluid behaviour and also a greater tendency to form phenocrysts. Higher iron and magnesium tends to manifest as a darker groundmass, and also occasionally amphibole or pyroxene phenocrysts.

Mafic Lava

Mafic or basaltic lavas are typified by their high ferromagnesian content, and generally erupt at temperatures in excess of 950° C. Basaltic magma is high in iron and magnesium, and has relatively lower aluminium and silica, which taken together reduces the degree of polymerization within the melt. Owing to the higher temperatures, viscosities can be relatively low, although still thousands of times more viscous than water. The low degree of polymerization and high temperature favors chemical diffusion, so it is common to see large, well-formed phenocrysts within mafic lavas. Basalt lavas tend to produce low-profile shield volcanoes or 'flood basalt fields', because the fluidal lava flows for long distances from the vent. The thickness of a basalt lava, particularly on a low slope, may be much greater than the thickness of the moving lava flow at any one time, because basalt lavas may 'inflate' by supply of lava beneath a solidified crust. Most basalt lavas are of *A a* or *pahoehoe* types, rather than block lavas. Underwater they can form 'pillow lavas', which are rather similar to entrail-type pahoehoe lavas on land.

Ultramafic Lava

Ultramafic lavas such as komatiite and highly magnesian magmas which form boninite take the composition and temperatures of eruptions to the extreme. Komatiites contain over 18 per cent magnesium oxide, and are thought to have erupted at temperatures of 1600° C. At this temperature there is no polymerization of the mineral compounds, creating a highly mobile liquid with viscosity as low as that of water. Most if not all ultramafic lavas are no younger than the Proterozoic, with a few ultramafic magmas known from the Phanerozoic. No modern komatiite lavas are known, as the Earth's mantle has cooled too much to produce highly magnesian magmas.

Lava Behaviour

The viscosity of lava is important because it determines how the lava will behave. Lavas with high viscosity are rhyolite, dacite, andesite and trachyte, with cooled basaltic lava also quite viscous; those with low viscosities are freshly erupted basalt, carbonatite and occasionally andesite.

Highly viscous lava shows the following behaviours:

- tends to flow slowly, clog, and form semi-solid blocks which resist flow;
- tends to entrap gas, which form vesicles (bubbles) within the rock as they rise to the surface;
- correlates with explosive or phreatic eruptions and is associated with tuff and pyroclastic flows.

Highly viscous lavas do not usually flow as liquid, and usually form explosive fragmental ash or tephra deposits. However, a degassed viscous lava or one which erupts somewhat hotter than usual may form a lava flow.

Lava with low viscosity shows the following behaviours:

- tends to flow easily, forming puddles, channels, and rivers of molten rock;
- tends to easily release bubbling gases as they are formed;
- eruptions are rarely pyroclastic and are usually quiescent; and
- volcanoes tend to form broad shields rather than steep cones.

Lavas also may contain many other components, sometimes including solid crystals of various minerals, fragments of exotic rocks known as xenoliths and fragments of previously solidified lava.

The physical behaviour of lava creates the physical forms of a lava flow or volcano. More fluid basaltic lava flows tend to form flat sheet-like bodies, whereas viscous rhyolite lava flows forms knobbly, blocky masses of rock.

General features of volcanology can be used to classify volcanic edifices and provide information on the eruptions which formed the lava flow, even if the sequence of lavas have been buried or metamorphosed.

The ideal lava flow will have a brecciated top, either as pillow lava development, autobreccia and rubble typical of *?a?a* and viscous flows, or a vesicular or frothy carapace such as scoria or pumice. The top of the lava will tend to be glassy, having been flash frozen in contact with the air or water.

The centre of a lava flow is commonly massive and crystalline, flow banded or layered, with microscopic groundmass crystals. The more viscous lava forms tend to show sheeted flow features, and blocks or breccia entrained within the sticky lava. The crystal size at the centre of a lava will in general be greater than at the margins, as the crystals have more time to grow.

The base of a lava flow may show evidence of hydrothermal activity if the lava flowed across moist or wet substrates. The lower part of the lava may have vesicles, perhaps filled with minerals (amygdules). The substrate upon which the lava has flowed may show signs of scouring, it may be broken or disturbed by the boiling of trapped water, and in the case of soil profiles, may be baked into a brick-red terracotta.

Discriminating between an intrusive sill and a lava flow in ancient rock sequences can be difficult. However, some sills do not usually have brecciated margins, and may show a weak metamorphic aureole on both the upper and lower surface, whereas a lava will only bake the substrate beneath it. However, it is often difficult in practise to identify these metamorphic phenomenon because they are usually weak and restricted in size. Peperitic sills intruded into wet sedimentary rocks, commonly do not bake upper margins and have upper and lower autobreccias, closely similar to lavas.

A a

A a (also spelled *aa,* , and *a-aa*; pronounced, from Hawaiian meaning 'stony rough lava', but also to 'burn' or 'blaze') is one of three basic types of flow lava. A a is basaltic lava characterized by a rough or rubbly surface composed of broken lava blocks called clinker. The Hawaiian word was introduced as a technical term in geology by Clarence Dutton.

The loose, broken, and sharp, spiny surface of an ?a?a flow makes hiking difficult and slow. The clinkery surface actually covers a massive dense core, which is the most active part of the flow. As pasty lava in the core travels downslope, the clinkers are carried along at the surface. At the leading edge of an ?a?a flow, however, these cooled fragments tumble down the steep front and are buried by the advancing flow. This produces a layer of lava fragments both at the bottom and top of an ?a?a flow.

Accretionary lava balls as large as 3 metres (10 feet) are common on a flows. *A a* is usually of higher viscosity than pahoehoe. Pahoehoe can turn into a a if it becomes turbulent from meeting impediments or steep slopes.

The sharp, angled texture makes *a a* a strong radar reflector, and can easily be seen from an orbiting satellite (bright on Magellan pictures).

A a lavas typically erupt at temperatures of 1000 to 1100° C.

Pahoehoe

Pahoehoe (also spelled *pahoehoe*, pronounced/from Hawaiian, meaning 'smooth, unbroken lava') is basaltic lava that has a smooth, billowy, undulating, or ropy surface. These surface features are due to the movement of very fluid lava under a congealing surface crust. The Hawaiian word was introduced as a technical term in geology by Clarence Dutton.

A pahoehoe flow typically advances as a series of small lobes and toes that continually break out from a cooled crust. It also forms lava tubes where the minimal heat loss maintains low viscosity. The surface texture of pahoehoe flows varies widely, displaying all kinds of bizarre shapes often referred to as lava sculpture. With increasing distance from the source, pahoehoe flows may change into a a flows in response to heat loss and consequent increase in viscosity. Pahoehoe lavas typically have a temperature of 1100 to 1200° C.

The rounded texture makes pahoehoe a poor radar reflector, and is difficult to see from an orbiting satellite.

Pillow lava is the lava structure typically formed when lava emerges from an underwater volcanic vent or subglacial volcano or a lava flow enters the ocean. However, pillow lava can also form when lava is erupted beneath thick glacial ice. The viscous lava gains a solid crust on contact with the water, and this crust cracks and oozes additional large blobs or 'pillows' as more lava emerges from the advancing flow. Since water covers the majority of Earth's surface and most volcanoes are situated near or under bodies of water, pillow lava is very common.

Volcanoes are the primary landforms built by repeated eruptions of lava and ash over time. They range in shape from shield volcanoes with broad, shallow slopes formed from predominantly effusive eruptions of relatively fluid basaltic lava flows, to steeply-sided stratovolcanoes (also known as composite volcanoes) made of alternating layers of ash and more viscous lava flows typical of intermediate and felsic lavas.

A caldera, which is a large subsidence crater, can form in a stratovolcano, if the magma chamber is partially or wholly emptied by large explosive eruptions; the summit cone no longer supports itself and thus collapses in on itself afterwards. Such features may include volcanic crater lakes and lava domes after the event. However, calderas can also form by non-explosive means such as gradual magma subsidence. This is typical of many shield volcanoes.

Cinder and Spatter Cones

Cinder cones and spatter cones are small-scale features formed by lava accumulation around a small vent on a volcanic edifice. Cinder cones are formed from tephra or ash and tuff which is thrown from an explosive vent. Spatter cones are formed by accumulation of molten volcanic slag and cinders ejected in a more liquid form.

Kipukas

Another Hawaiian English term derived from the Hawaiian language, a kipuka denotes an elevated area such as a hill, ridge or old lava dome inside or downslope from an area of active volcanism. New lava flows will cover the surrounding land, isolating the kipuka so that it appears as a (usually) forested island in a barren lava flow.

Lava Domes

Lava domes are formed by the extrusion of viscous felsic magma. They can form prominent rounded protuberances, such as at Valles Caldera. As a volcano extrudes silicic lava, it can form an *inflation dome*, gradually building up a large, pillow-like structure which cracks, fissures, and may release cooled chunks of rock and rubble. The top and side margins of an inflating lava dome tend to be covered in fragments of rock, breccia and ash.

Examples of lava dome eruptions include the Novarupta dome, and successive lava domes of Mount St Helens.

Lava Tubes

Lava tubes are formed when a flow of relatively fluid lava cools on the upper surface sufficiently to form a crust. Beneath this crust, which being made of rock is an excellent insulator, the lava can continue to flow as a liquid. When this flow occurs over a prolonged period of time the lava conduit can form a tunnel-like aperture or *lava tube*, which can conduct molten rock many kilometres from the vent without cooling appreciably. Often these lava tubes drain out once the supply of fresh lava has stopped, leaving a considerable length of open tunnel within the lava flow.

Lava tubes are known from the modern day eruptions of Kilauea, and significant, extensive and open lava tubes of Tertiary age are known from North Queensland, Australia, some extending for 15 kilometres.

Lava Cascades and Fountains

The eruptions of lava are sometimes attended by peculiarities which impart to them much additional grandeur. Instances have occurred in which the molten stream has plunged over a sheer precipice of immense height, so as to produce a glowing cascade exceeding (in breadth and perpendicular descent) the celebrated Niagara Falls. In other cases, the lava, instead of at once flowing down the sides of the mountain, has been first thrown up into the air as a lava fountain up to several hundred metres in height.

Lava flows are enormously destructive to property in their path but generally move slowly enough for people to get out of their way, though this is dependent on the viscosity of the lava; casualties caused directly by active lava flows are rare. Nevertheless injuries and deaths have occurred, either because people had their escape route cut off, because they got too close to the flow or, more rarely, if the lava flow front travelled too quickly. This notably happened during the eruption of Nyiragongo in Zaire (now Democratic Republic of Congo) on 10 January 1977 when the crater wall was breached during the night and the fluid lava lake in it drained out in less than an hour. Flowing down the steep slopes of the volcano at up to 100 km/h, the lava swiftly overwhelmed several villages whilst their residents were asleep. As a result of this disaster, the mountain was designated a Decade Volcano in 1991.

Deaths attributed to volcanoes frequently have a different cause, for example volcanic ejecta, pyroclastic flow from a collapsing lava dome, lahars, poisonous gases that travel ahead of lava, or explosions caused when the flow comes into contact with water.

6 Rock

In geology, rock or stone is a naturally occurring solid aggregate of minerals and/or mineraloids.

The Earth's outer solid layer, the lithosphere, is made of rock. In general rocks are of three types, namely, igneous, sedimentary, and metamorphic. The scientific study of rocks is called petrology, and petrology is an essential component of geology.

Rocks are generally classified by mineral and chemical composition, by the texture of the constituent particles and by the processes that formed them. These indicators separate rocks into igneous, sedimentary, and metamorphic. They are further classified according to particle size. The transformation of one rock type to another is described by the geological model called the rock cycle.

Igneous rocks are formed when molten magma cools and are divided into two main categories: plutonic rock and volcanic. Plutonic or intrusive rocks result when magma cools and crystallizes slowly within the Earth's crust (example granite), while volcanic or extrusive rocks result from magma reaching the surface either as lava or fragmental ejecta.

Sedimentary rocks are formed by deposition of either clastic sediments, organic matter, or chemical precipitates (evaporites), followed by compaction of the particulate matter and cementation during diagenesis. Sedimentary rocks form at or near the Earth's surface. Mud rocks comprise 65 per cent (mudstone, shale and siltstone); sandstones 20 to 25 per cent and carbonate rocks 10 to 15 per cent (limestone and dolostone).

Metamorphic rocks are formed by subjecting any rock type (including previously formed metamorphic rock) to different temperature and pressure conditions than those in which the original rock was formed. These temperatures and pressures are always higher than those at the Earth's surface and must be sufficiently high so as to change the original minerals into other mineral types or else into other forms of the same minerals (e.g. by recrystallisation).

The three classes of rocks — the igneous, the sedimentary and the metamorphic — are subdivided into many groups. There are, however, no hard and fast boundaries between allied rocks. By increase or decrease in the proportions of their constituent minerals they pass by every gradation into one another, the distinctive structures also of one kind of rock may often be traced gradually merging into those of another. Hence the definitions adopted in establishing rock nomenclature merely correspond to selected points (more or less arbitrary) in a continuously graduated series.

The use of rocks has had a huge impact on the cultural and technological development of the human race. Rocks have been used by humans and other hominids for more than 2 million years. Lithic technology marks some of the oldest and continuously used technologies. The mining of rocks for their metal ore content has been one of the most important factors of human advancement, which has progressed at different rates in different places in part because of the kind of metals available from the rocks of a region.

The prehistory and history of civilization is classified into the Stone Age, Bronze Age, and Iron Age. Although the stone age has ended virtually everywhere, rocks continue to be used to construct buildings and infrastructure. When so used, rocks are called dimension stone.

Formation of Rocks

The three main ways rocks are formed:

1. Sedimentary rocks are formed through the gradual accumulation of sediment: for example, sand on a beach or mud on a river bed. As the sediment is buried it is compacted as more and more material is deposited on top. Eventually the sediment will become so dense that it is essentially rock. This process is known as lithification.
2. Igneous rocks are rocks which have crystallized from a melt or magma. The melt is made up of various components of pre-existing rocks which have been subjected to melting either at subduction zones or within the Earth's mantle. The melt is hot and so passes upward through cooler country rock. As it moves it cools and various rock types will form through a process known as fractional crystallization. Igneous rocks can be seen at mid ocean ridges, areas of island arc volcanism or in intra-plate hotspots.
3. Metamorphic rocks are rocks which once existed as igneous or sedimentary rocks but have been subjected to varying degrees of pressure and heat within the Earth's crust. The processes involved will change the composition and fabric of the rock and their original nature is often hard to distinguish. Metamorphic rocks are typically found in areas of mountain building.

Rock Synthesis

The synthetic investigation of rocks proceeds by experimental work that attempts to reproduce different rock types and to elucidate their origins and structures. In many cases no experiment is necessary. Every stage in the origin of clays, sands and gravels can be seen in process around us, but where these have been converted into coherent shales, sandstone and conglomerates, and still more where they have experienced some degree of metamorphism, there are many obscure points about their history upon which experiment may yet throw light. Attempts have been made to reproduce igneous rocks, by fusion of mixtures of crushed minerals or of chemicals in specially contrived furnaces. The earliest researches of this sort are those of Faujas St Fond and of de Saussure, but Sir James Hall really laid the foundations of this branch of petrology. He showed (1798) that the whinstones (diabases) of Edinburgh were fusible and if rapidly cooled yielded black vitreous masses closely resembling natural pitchstones and obsidians, if cooled more slowly they consolidated as crystalline rocks not unlike the whinstones themselves and containing olivine, augite and feldspar (the essential minerals of these rocks).

Many years later Daubrée, Delesse and others carried on similar experiments, but the first notable advance was made in 1878, when Fouqué and Lévy began their researches. They succeeded in producing such rocks as porphyrite, leucite-tephrite, basalt and dolerite, and obtained also various structural modifications well known in igneous rocks, e.g. the porphyritic and the ophitic. Incidentally they showed that while many basic rocks (basalts, etc.) could be perfectly imitated in the laboratory, the acid rocks could not, and advanced the explanation that for the crystallization of the latter the gases never absent in natural rock magmas were indispensable mineralizing agents. It has subsequently been proved that steam, or such volatile substances as certain borates, molybdates, chlorides, fluorides, assist in the formation of orthoclase, quartz and mica (the minerals of granite). Sir James Hall also made the first contribution to the experimental study of metamorphic rocks by converting chalk into marble by heating it in a closed gun-barrel, which prevented the escape of the carbonic acid at high temperatures. In 1901 Adams and Nicholson carried this a stage further by subjecting marble to great pressures in hydraulic presses and have shown how the foliated structures, frequent in natural marbles, may be produced artificially.

Rock Cycle

The rock cycle is a fundamental concept in geology that describes the dynamic transitions through geologic time among the three main rock types: sedimentary, metamorphic, and igneous. As the diagram to the right illustrates, each type of rock is altered or destroyed when it is forced out of its equilibrium conditions. An igneous rock such as basalt may break down and dissolve when exposed to the atmosphere, or melt as it is subducted under a continent. Due to the driving forces of the rock cycle, plate tectonics and the water cycle, rocks do not remain in equilibrium and are forced to change as they encounter new environments. The rock cycle is an illustration that explains how the three rock types are related to each other and how processes change from one type to another over time.

The original concept of the *rock cycle* is usually attributed to James Hutton, from the eighteenth century *father of geology*. The rock cycle was a part of Hutton's *uniformitarianism* and his famous quote: *no vestige of a beginning, and no prospect of an end*, applied in particular to the rock cycle and the envisioned cyclical nature of geologic processes. This concept of a repetitive non-evolutionary rock cycle remained dominant until the plate tectonics revolution of the 1960s. With the developing understanding of the driving *engine* of plate tectonics, the rock cycle changed from endlessly repetitive to a gradually evolving process. The *Wilson cycle* (a plate tectonics based rock cycle) was developed by J. Tuzo Wilson during the 1950s and 1960s.

Transition to Igneous

When rocks are pushed deep under the Earth's surface, they may melt into magma. If the conditions no longer exist for the magma to stay in its liquid state, it will cool and solidify into an igneous rock. A rock that cools within the Earth is called intrusive or plutonic and will cool very slowly, producing a coarse-grained texture. As a result of volcanic activity, magma (which is called lava when it reaches Earth's surface) may cool very rapidly while being on Earth's surface exposed to the atmosphere and are called extrusive or volcanic rocks. These rocks are fine-grained and sometimes cool so rapidly that no crystals can form and result in a natural glass, such as obsidian. Any of the three main types of rocks (igneous, sedimentary, and metamorphic rocks) can melt into magma and cool into igneous rocks.

Post-volcanic Changes

Rock masses of igneous origin have no sooner cooled than they begin to change. The gases with which the magma is charged are slowly dissipated, lava flows often remain hot and steaming for many years. These gases attack the components of the rock and deposit new minerals in cavities and fissures. The zeolites are largely of this origin. Even before these 'post-volcanic' processes have ceased, atmospheric decomposition or weathering begins as the mineral components of volcanic and igneous rocks are not stable under surface atmospheric conditions. Rain, frost, carbonic acid, oxygen and other agents operate continuously, and do not cease until the whole mass has crumbled down and most of its ingredients have been resolved into new products or carried away in aqueous solution. In the classification of rocks these secondary changes are generally considered unessential: rocks are classified and described as if they were ideally fresh, though this is rarely the case in nature.

Secondary Changes

Epigenetic change (secondary processes) may be arranged under a number of headings, each of which is typical of a group of rocks or rock-forming minerals, though usually more than one of these alterations will be found in progress in the same rock. Silicification, the replacement of the minerals by crystalline or crypto-crystalline silica, is most common in felsic rocks, such as rhyolite, but is also found in serpentine, etc. Kaolinization is the decomposition of the feldspars, which are the most common minerals in igneous rocks, into kaolin (along with quartz and other clay minerals); it is best shown by granites and syenites. Serpentinization is the alteration of olivine to serpentine (with magnetite); it is typical of peridotites, but occurs in most of the mafic rocks. In uralitization secondary hornblende replaces augite; this occurs very generally in diabases; chloritization is the alteration of augite (biotite or hornblende) to chlorite, and is seen in many diabases, diorites and greenstones. Epidotization occurs also in rocks of this group, and consists in the development of epidote from biotite, hornblende, augite or plagioclase feldspar.

Transition to Metamorphic

Rocks exposed to high temperatures and/or pressures can be changed physically or chemically to form a different rock, called metamorphic. Regional metamorphism refers to the effects on large masses of rocks over a wide area, typically associated with mountain building events within orogenic belts. These rocks commonly exhibit distinct bands of differing mineralogy and colours, called foliation. Another main type of metamorphism is caused when a body of rock comes into contact with an igneous intrusion that heats up this surrounding country rock. This *contact metamorphism* results in a rock that is altered and re-crystallized by the extreme heat of the magma and/or by the addition of fluids from the magma that add chemicals to the surrounding rock (metasomatism). Any pre-existing type of rock can be modified by the processes of metamorphism.

Transition to Sedimentary

Rocks exposed to the atmosphere are variably unstable and subject to the processes of weathering and erosion. Weathering and erosion breaks the original rock down into smaller fragments and carries away dissolved material. This fragmented material accumulates and is buried by additional material. While an individual grain of sand is still a member of the class of rock it was formed from, a rock made up of such grains fused together is sedimentary. Sedimentary rocks can be formed from the lithification of these buried smaller fragments (clastic sedimentary rock), the accumulation and lithification of material generated by living organisms (biogenic sedimentary rock-fossils), or lithification of chemically precipitated material from a mineral bearing solution due to evaporation (precipitate sedimentary rock). Clastic rocks can be formed from fragments broken apart from larger rocks of any type, due to processes such as erosion or from organic material, like plant remains. Biogenic and precipitate rocks form from the deposition of minerals from chemicals dissolved from all other rock types.

Plate Tectonics

In 1967, J. Tuzo Wilson published an article in Nature describing the repeated opening and closing of ocean basins, in particular focussing on the current Atlantic Ocean area. This concept, a part of the plate tectonics revolution, became known as the *Wilson cycle*. The Wilson cycle has had profound effects on the modern interpretation of the rock cycle as Plate tectonics became recognized as the driving force for the rock cycle.

Spreading Ridges

The *start* of the cycle can be placed at the mid-ocean divergent boundaries where new magma is produced by mantle upwelling and a shallow *melting zone*. This *new* or *juvenile* basaltic magma is the first phase of the igneous portion of the cycle. It should be noted that the least dense magma phases tend to be favored in eruptions. As the ridge *spreads* and the new rock is carried away from the ridge, the interaction of heated circulating seawater through crevices starts the initial *retrograde* metamorphism of the new rock.

Subduction Zones

The new basaltic oceanic crust eventually meets a subduction zone as it moves away from the spreading ridge. As this crust is pulled back into the mantle, the increasing pressure and temperature conditions cause a restructuring of the mineralogy of the rock, this metamorphism alters the rock to form eclogite. As the slab of basaltic crust and some included sediments are dragged deeper, water and other more volatile materials are driven off and rise into the overlying wedge of rock above the subduction zone which is at a lower pressure. The lower pressure, high temperature, and now volatile rich material in this wedge melts and the resulting buoyant magma rises through the overlying rock to produce island arc or continental margin volcanism. This volcanism includes more silicic lavas the further from the edge of the island arc or continental margin, indicating a deeper source and a more differentiated magma.

At times some of the metamorphosed downgoing slab may be thrust up or obducted onto the continental margin. These blocks of mantle peridotite and the metamorphic eclogites are exposed as ophiolite complexes.

The newly erupted volcanic material is subject to rapid erosion depending on the climate conditions. These sediments accumulate within the basins on either side of an island arc. As the sediments become more deeply buried lithification begins and sedimentary rock results.

Continental Collision

On the closing phase of the classic Wilson cycle, two continental or smaller terranes meet at a convergent zone. As the two masses of continental crust meet, neither can be subducted as they are both *low density* silicic rock. As the two masses meet, tremendous compressional forces distort and modify the rocks involved. The result is regional metamorphism within the interior of the ensuing orogeny or mountain building event. As the two masses are compressed, folded and faulted into a mountain range by the continental collision the whole suite of pre-existing igneous, volcanic, sedimentary and earlier metamorphic rock units are subjected to this new metamorphic event.

Accelerated Erosion

The high mountain ranges produced by continental collisions are immediately subjected to the forces of erosion. Erosion wears down the mountains and massive piles of sediment are developed in adjacent ocean margins, shallow seas, and as continental deposits. As these sediment piles are buried deeper they become lithified into sedimentary rock. The metamorphic, igneous, and sedimentary rocks of the mountains become the new piles of sediments in the adjoining basins and eventually become sedimentary rock.

An Evolving Process

The plate tectonics rock cycle is an evolutionary process. Magma generation, both in the spreading ridge environment and within the wedge above a subduction zone, favours the eruption of the more silicic and volatile rich fraction of the crustal or upper mantle material. This lower density material tends to stay within the crust and not be subducted back into the mantle. The magmatic aspects of plate tectonics tends to gradual segregation within or between the mantle and crust. As magma forms, the initial melt is composed of the more silicic phases that have a lower melting point. This leads to partial melting and further segregation of the lithosphere. In addition the silicic continental crust is relatively buoyant and is not normally subducted back into the mantle. So over time the continental masses grow larger and larger.

The Role of Water

The presence of abundant water on Earth is of great importance for the rock cycle. Most obvious perhaps are the water driven processes of weathering and erosion. Water in the form of precipitation and acidic soil water and groundwater is quite effective at dissolving minerals and rocks, especially those igneous and metamorphic rocks and marine sedimentary rocks that are unstable under near surface and atmospheric conditions. The water carries away the ions dissolved in solution and the broken down fragments that are the products of weathering. Running water carries vast amounts of sediment in rivers back to the ocean and inland basins. The accumulated and buried sediments are converted back into rock.

A less obvious role of water is in the metamorphism processes that occur in fresh seafloor volcanic rocks as seawater, sometimes heated, flows through the fractures and crevices in the rock. All of these processes, illustrated by serpentinization, are an important part of the destruction of volcanic rock.

The role of water and other volatiles in the melting of existing crustal rock in the wedge above a subduction zone is a most important part of the cycle. Along with water, the presence of carbon dioxide and other carbon compounds from abundant marine limestone within the sediments atop the downgoing slab is another source of melt inducing volatiles. This involves the carbon cycle as a part of the overall rock cycle.

Lithosphere

The lithosphere (pronounced from the Greek [*lithos*] for 'rocky' + sfa [*sphaira*] for 'sphere') is the rigid outermost shell of a rocky planet. It comprises the crust and the portion of the upper mantle that behaves elastically on time scales of thousands of years or greater.

In the Earth, the lithosphere includes the crust and the uppermost mantle, which constitute the hard and rigid outer layer of the Earth. The lithosphere is underlain by the asthenosphere, the weaker, hotter, and deeper part of the upper mantle. The boundary between the lithosphere and the underlying asthenosphere is defined by a difference in response to stress: the lithosphere remains rigid for very long periods of geologic time in which it deforms elastically and through brittle failure, while the asthenosphere deforms viscously and accommodates strain through plastic deformation. The lithosphere is broken into tectonic plates. The uppermost part of the lithosphere that chemically reacts to the atmosphere, hydrosphere and biosphere through the soil forming process is called the pedosphere.

The concept of the lithosphere as Earth's strong outer layer was developed by Joseph Barrell, who wrote a series of papers introducing the concept. The concept was based on the presence of significant gravity anomalies over continental crust, from which he inferred that there must exist a strong upper layer (which he called the lithosphere) above a weaker layer which could flow (which he called the asthenosphere). These ideas were expanded by Daly (1940) , and have been broadly accepted by geologists and geophysicists. Although these ideas about lithosphere and asthenosphere were developed long before plate tectonic theory was articulated in the 1960s, the concepts that a strong lithosphere exists and that this rests on a weak asthenosphere are essential to that theory. The lithosphere provides a conductive lid atop the convecting mantle; as such, it affects heat transport through the Earth.

The lithosphere provides a conductive lid atop the convecting mantle; as such, it affects heat transport through the Earth.

There are two types of lithosphere:

1. Oceanic lithosphere, which is associated with Oceanic crust and exists in the ocean basins
2. Continental lithosphere, which is associated with Continental crust.

The thickness of the lithosphere is considered to be the depth to the isotherm associated with the transition between brittle and viscous behaviour . The temperature at which olivine begins to deform viscously (~1000° C) is often used to set this isotherm because olivine is generally the weakest mineral in the upper mantle. Oceanic lithosphere is typically about 50-100 km thick (but beneath the mid-ocean ridges is no thicker than the crust), while continental lithosphere has a range in thickness from about 40 km to perhaps 200 km; the upper ~30 to ~50 km of typical continental lithosphere is crust. The mantle part of the lithosphere consists largely of peridotite. The crust is distinguished from the upper mantle by the change in chemical composition that takes place at the Moho discontinuity.

Oceanic Lithosphere

Oceanic lithosphere consists mainly of mafic crust and ultramafic mantle (peridotite) and is denser than continental lithosphere, for which the mantle is associated with crust made of felsic rocks. Oceanic lithosphere thickens as it ages and moves away from the mid-ocean ridge. This thickening occurs by conductive cooling, which converts hot asthenosphere into lithospheric mantle, and causes the oceanic lithosphere to become increasingly thick and dense with age. The thickness of the mantle part of the oceanic lithosphere can be approximated as a thermal boundary layer that thickens as the square root of time.

Oceanic lithosphere is less dense than asthenosphere for a few tens of millions of years, but after this becomes increasingly denser than asthenosphere. This is because the chemically-differentiated oceanic crust is lighter than asthenosphere, but due to thermal contraction, the mantle lithosphere is more dense than the asthenosphere. The gravitational instability of mature oceanic lithosphere has the effect that at subduction zones, oceanic lithosphere invariably sinks underneath the overriding lithosphere, which can be oceanic or continental. New oceanic lithosphere is constantly being produced at mid-ocean ridges and is recycled back to the mantle at subduction zones. As a result, oceanic lithosphere is much younger than continental lithosphere: the oldest oceanic lithosphere is about 170 million years old, while parts of the continental lithosphere are billions of years old. The oldest parts of continental lithosphere underlie cratons, and the mantle lithosphere there is thicker and less dense than typical; the relatively low density of such mantle 'roots of cratons' helps to stabilize these regions.

Subducted Lithosphere

Geophysical studies in the early 21st Century posit that large pieces of the lithosphere have been subducted into the mantle as deep as 2900 km to near the core-mantle boundary , while others 'float' in the upper mantle, while some stick down into the mantle as far as 400 km but remain 'attached' to the continental plate above, similar to the extent of the 'tectosphere' proposed by Jordan in 1988.

Mantle Xenoliths

Geoscientists can directly study the nature of the subcontinental mantle by examining mantle xenoliths brought up in kimberlite, lamproite, and other volcanic pipes. The histories of these xenoliths have been investigated by many methods, including analyses of abundances of isotopes of osmium and rhenium. Such studies have confirmed that mantle lithospheres below some cratons have persisted for periods in excess of 3 billion years, despite the mantle flow that accompanies plate tectonics.

7 Igneous Rock

Igneous rock (derived from the Latin word *igneus* meaning of fire, from *ignis* meaning fire) is one of the three main rock types, the others being sedimentary and metamorphic rock. Igneous rock is formed through the cooling and solidification of magma or lava. Igneous rock may form with or without crystallization, either below the surface as intrusive (plutonic) rocks or on the surface as extrusive (volcanic) rocks. This magma can be derived from partial melts of pre-existing rocks in either a planet's mantle or crust. Typically, the melting is caused by one or more of three processes: an increase in temperature, a decrease in pressure, or a change in composition. Over 700 types of igneous rocks have been described, most of them having formed beneath the surface of Earth's crust. These have diverse properties, depending on their composition and how they were formed.

The upper 16 kilometres (10 mi) of Earth's crust is composed of approximately 95 per cent igneous rocks with only a thin, widespread covering of sedimentary and metamorphic rocks.

Igneous rocks are geologically important because:

- which some igneous rocks are extracted, and the temperature and pressure conditions that allowed this extraction, and/or of other pre-existing rock that melted;
- their absolute ages can be obtained from various forms of radiometric dating and thus can be compared to adjacent geological strata, allowing a time sequence of events;
- their features are usually characteristic of a specific tectonic environment, allowing tectonic reconstitutions;
- in some special circumstances they host important mineral deposits (ores): for example, tungsten, tin, and uranium are commonly associated with granites and diorites, whereas ores of chromium and platinum are commonly associated with gabbros.

Intrusive Igneous Rocks

Intrusive igneous rocks are formed from magma that cools and solidifies within the crust of a planet. Surrounded by pre-existing rock (called country rock), the magma cools slowly, and as a result these rocks are coarse grained. The mineral grains in such rocks can generally be identified with the naked eye. Intrusive rocks can also be classified according to the shape and size of the intrusive body and its relation to the other formations into which it intrudes. Typical intrusive formations are batholiths, stocks, laccoliths, sills and dikes.

The central cores of major mountain ranges consist of intrusive igneous rocks, usually granite. When exposed by erosion, these cores (called *batholiths*) may occupy huge areas of the Earth's surface.

Coarse grained intrusive igneous rocks which form at depth within the crust are termed as *abyssal*; intrusive igneous rocks which form near the surface are termed *hypabyssal*.

Extrusive Igneous Rocks

Extrusive igneous rocks are formed at the crust's surface as a result of the partial melting of rocks within the mantle and crust. Extrusive Igneous rocks cool and solidify quicker than intrusive igneous rocks. Since the rocks cool very quickly they are fine grained.

The melted rock, with or without suspended crystals and gas bubbles, is called magma. Magma rises because it is less dense than the rock from which it was created. When it reaches the surface, magma extruded onto the surface either beneath water or air, is called lava. Eruptions of volcanoes into air are termed *subaerial* whereas those occurring underneath the ocean are termed *submarine.* Black smokers and mid-ocean ridge basalt are examples of submarine volcanic activity.

The volume of extrusive rock erupted annually by volcanoes varies with plate tectonic setting. Extrusive rock is produced in the following proportions:

- divergent boundary: 73 per cent
- convergent boundary (subduction zone): 15 per cent
- hotspot: 12 per cent.

Magma which erupts from a volcano behaves according to its viscosity, determined by temperature, composition, and crystal content. High-temperature magma, most of which is basaltic in composition, behaves in a manner similar to thick oil and, as it cools, treacle. Long, thin basalt flows with pahoehoe surfaces are common. Intermediate composition magma such as andesite tends to form cinder cones of intermingled ash, tuff and lava, and may have viscosity similar to thick, cold molasses or even rubber when erupted. Felsic magma such as rhyolite is usually erupted at low temperature and is up to 10,000 times as viscous as basalt. Volcanoes with rhyolitic magma commonly erupt explosively, and rhyolitic lava flows typically are of limited extent and have steep margins, because the magma is so viscous.

Felsic and intermediate magmas that erupt often do so violently, with explosions driven by release of dissolved gases — typically water but also carbon dioxide. Explosively erupted pyroclastic material is called tephra and includes tuff, agglomerate and ignimbrite. Fine volcanic ash is also erupted and forms ash tuff deposits which can often cover vast areas.

Because lava cools and crystallizes rapidly, it is fine grained. If the cooling has been so rapid as to prevent the formation of even small crystals after extrusion, the resulting rock may be mostly glass (such as the rock obsidian). If the cooling of the lava happened slowly, the rocks would be coarse-grained.

Because the minerals are mostly fine-grained, it is much more difficult to distinguish between the different types of extrusive igneous rocks than between different types of intrusive igneous rocks. Generally, the mineral constituents of fine-grained extrusive igneous rocks can only be determined by examination of thin sections of the rock under a microscope, so only an approximate classification can usually be made in the field.

Hypabyssal Igneous Rocks

Hypabyssal igneous rocks are formed at a depth in between the plutonic and volcanic rocks. Hypabyssal rocks are less common than plutonic or volcanic rocks and do often form dikes, sills or laccoliths.

Classification

Igneous rocks are classified according to mode of occurrence, texture, mineralogy, chemical composition, and the geometry of the igneous body.

The classification of the many types of different igneous rocks can provide us with important information about the conditions under which they formed. Two important variables used for the classification of igneous rocks are particle size, which largely depends upon the cooling history, and the mineral composition of the rock. Feldspars, quartz or feldspathoids, olivines, pyroxenes, amphiboles, and micas are all important minerals in the formation of almost all igneous rocks, and they are basic to the classification of these rocks. All other minerals present are regarded as nonessential in almost all igneous rocks and are called *accessory minerals*. Types of igneous rocks with other essential minerals are very rare, and these rare rocks include those with essential carbonates.

In a simplified classification, igneous rock types are separated on the basis of the type of feldspar present, the presence or absence of quartz, and in rocks with no feldspar or quartz, the type of iron or magnesium minerals present. Rocks containing quartz (silica in composition) are silica-oversaturated. Rocks with feldspathoids are silica-undersaturated, because feldspathoids cannot coexist in a stable association with quartz.

Igneous rocks which have crystals large enough to be seen by the naked eye are called phaneritic; those with crystals too small to be seen are called aphanitic. Generally speaking, phaneritic implies an intrusive origin; aphanitic an extrusive one.

An igneous rock with larger, clearly discernible crystals embedded in a finer-grained matrix is termed porphyry. Porphyritic texture develops when some of the crystals grow to considerable size before the main mass of the magma crystallizes as finer-grained, uniform material.

Texture

Texture is an important criterion for the naming of volcanic rocks. The texture of volcanic rocks, including the size, shape, orientation, and distribution of mineral grains and the intergrain relationships, will determine whether the rock is termed a tuff, a pyroclastic lava or a simple lava.

However, the texture is only a subordinate part of classifying volcanic rocks, as most often there needs to be chemical information gleaned from rocks with extremely fine-grained groundmass or from airfall tuffs, which may be formed from volcanic ash.

Textural criteria are less critical in classifying intrusive rocks where the majority of minerals will be visible to the naked eye or at least using a hand lens, magnifying glass or microscope. Plutonic rocks tend also to be less texturally varied and less prone to gaining structural fabrics. Textural terms can be used to differentiate different intrusive phases of large plutons, for instance porphyritic margins to large intrusive bodies, porphyry stocks and subvolcanic dikes (apophyses). Mineralogical classification is used most often to classify plutonic rocks. Chemical classifications are preferred to classify volcanic rocks, with phenocryst species used as a prefix, e.g. “olivine-bearing picrite” or “orthoclase-phyric rhyolite”.

Chemical Classification

Igneous rocks can be classified according to chemical or mineralogical parameters:

- Chemical: total alkali-silica content (TAS diagram) for volcanic rock classification used when modal or mineralogic data is unavailable:
  - *acid* igneous rocks containing a high silica content, greater than 63 per cent SiO_2 (examples granite and rhyolite)
  - *intermediate* igneous rocks containing between 52-63 per cent SiO_2 (example andesite and dacite)
  - *basic* igneous rocks have low silica 45-52 per cent and typically high iron - magnesium content (example gabbro and basalt)
  - *ultrabasic* igneous rocks with less than 45 per cent silica. (examples picrite and komatiite)

— *alkalic* igneous rocks with 5-15 per cent alkali (K_2O + Na_2O) content or with a molar ratio of alkali to silica greater than 1:6. (examples phonolite and trachyte)

Note: the acid-basic terminology is used more broadly in older (generally British) geological literature. In current literature felsic-mafic roughly substitutes for acid-basic.

Chemical classification also extends to differentiating rocks which are chemically similar according to the TAS diagram, for instance:

- Ultrapotassic; rocks containing molar $K_2O/Na_2O > 3$
- Peralkaline; rocks containing molar $(K_2O + Na_2O)/Al_2O_3 > 1$
- Peraluminous; rocks containing molar $(K_2O + Na_2O)/Al_2O_3 < 1$

An idealized mineralogy (the normative mineralogy) can be calculated from the chemical composition, and the calculation is useful for rocks too fine-grained or too altered for identification of minerals that crystallized from the melt. For instance, normative quartz classifies a rock as silica-oversaturated; an example is rhyolite. A normative feldspathoid classifies a rock as silica-undersaturated; an example is nephelinite.

History of Classification

In 1902 a group of American petrographers proposed that all existing classifications of igneous rocks should be discarded and replaced by a "quantitative" classification based on chemical analysis. They showed how vague and often unscientific was much of the existing terminology and argued that as the chemical composition of an igneous rock was its most fundamental characteristic it should be elevated to prime position.

Geological occurrence, structure, mineralogical constitution–the hitherto accepted criteria for the discrimination of rock species–were relegated to the background. The completed rock analysis is first to be interpreted in terms of the rock-forming minerals which might be expected to be formed when the magma crystallizes, e.g., quartz feldspars, olivine, akermannite, feldspathoids, magnetite, corundum and so on, and the rocks are divided into groups strictly according to the Mineralogical classification.

For volcanic rocks, mineralogy is important in classifying and naming lavas. The most important criterion is the phenocryst species, followed by the groundmass mineralogy. Often, where the groundmass is aphanitic, chemical classification must be used to properly identify a volcanic rock.

Mineralogic Contents — Felsic *vs.* Mafic

- *felsic* rock, highest content of silicon, with predominance of quartz, alkali feldspar and/or feldspathoids: *the felsic minerals*; these rocks (e.g., granite, rhyolite) are usually light coloured, and have low density.
- *mafic* rock, lesser content of silicon relative to felsic rocks, with predominance of mafic minerals pyroxenes, olivines and calcic plagioclase; these rocks (example, basalt, gabbro) are usually dark coloured, and have a higher density than felsic rocks.
- *ultramafic* rock, lowest content of silicon, with more than 90 per cent of mafic minerals (e.g., dunite).

For intrusive, plutonic and usually phaneritic igneous rocks where all minerals are visible at least via microscope, the mineralogy is used to classify the rock. This usually occurs on ternary diagrams, where the relative proportions of three minerals are used to classify the rock.

Example of Classification

Granite is an igneous intrusive rock (crystallized at depth), with felsic composition (rich in silica and predominately quartz plus potassium-rich feldspar plus sodium-rich plagioclase) and phaneritic, subeuhedral texture (minerals are visible to the unaided eye and commonly some of them retain original crystallographic shapes).

Magma Origination

The Earth's crust averages about 35 kilometers thick under the continents, but averages only some 7-10 kilometers beneath the oceans. The continental crust is composed primarily of sedimentary rocks resting on crystalline *basement* formed of a great variety of metamorphic and igneous rocks including granulite and granite. Oceanic crust is composed primarily of basalt and gabbro. Both continental and oceanic crust rest on peridotite of the mantle.

Rocks may melt in response to a decrease in pressure, to a change in composition such as an addition of water, to an increase in temperature, or to a combination of these processes.

Other mechanisms, such as melting from impact of a meteorite, are less important today, but impacts during accretion of the Earth led to extensive melting, and the outer several hundred kilometers of our early Earth probably was an ocean of magma. Impacts of large meteorites in last few hundred million years have been proposed as one mechanism responsible for the extensive basalt magmatism of several large igneous provinces.

Decompression

Decompression melting occurs because of a decrease in pressure. The solidus temperatures of most rocks (the temperatures below which they are completely solid) increase with increasing pressure in the absence of water. Peridotite at depth in the Earth's mantle may be hotter than its solidus temperature at some shallower level. If such rock rises during the convection of solid mantle, it will cool slightly as it expands in an adiabatic process, but the cooling is only about 0.3°C per kilometer. Experimental studies of appropriate peridotite samples document that the solidus temperatures increase by 3°C to 4°C per kilometer. If the rock rises far enough, it will begin to melt. Melt droplets can coalesce into larger volumes and be intruded upwards. This process of melting from upward movement of solid mantle is critical in the evolution of Earth.

Decompression melting creates the ocean crust at mid-ocean ridges. Decompression melting caused by the rise of mantle plumes is responsible for creating ocean islands like the Hawaiian islands. Plume-related decompression melting also is the most common explanation for flood basalts and oceanic plateaus (two types of large igneous provinces), although other causes such as melting related to meteorite impact have been proposed for some of these huge volumes of igneous rock.

Effects of Water and Carbon Dioxide

The change of rock composition most responsible for creation of magma is the addition of water. Water lowers the solidus temperature of rocks at a given pressure. For example, at a depth of about 100 kilometers, peridotite begins to melt near 800°C in the presence of excess water, but near or above about 1500°C in the absence of water. Water is driven out of the oceanic lithosphere in subduction zones, and it causes melting in the overlying mantle. Hydrous magmas of basalt and andesite composition are produced directly and indirectly as results of dehydration during the subduction process. Such magmas and those derived from them build up island arcs such as those in the Pacific ring of fire. These magmas form rocks of the calc-alkaline series, an important part of continental crust.

The addition of carbon dioxide is relatively a much less important cause of magma formation than addition of water, but genesis of some silica-undersaturated magmas has been attributed to the dominance of carbon dioxide over water in their mantle source regions. In the presence of carbon dioxide, experiments document that the peridotite solidus temperature decreases by about 200° C in a narrow pressure interval at pressures corresponding to a depth of about 70 km. At greater depths, carbon dioxide can have more effect: at depths to about 200 km, the temperatures of initial melting of a carbonated peridotite composition were determined to be 450° C to 600° C lower than for the same composition with no carbon dioxide. Magmas of rock types such as nephelinite, carbonatite, and kimberlite are among those that may be generated following an influx of carbon dioxide into mantle at depths greater than about 70 km.

Temperature Increase

Increase of temperature is the most typical mechanism for formation of magma within continental crust. Such temperature increases can occur because of the upward intrusion of magma from the mantle. Temperatures can also exceed the solidus of a crustal rock in continental crust thickened by compression at a plate boundary. The plate boundary between the Indian and Asian continental masses provides a well-studied example, as the Tibetan Plateau just north of the boundary has crust about 80 kilometers thick, roughly twice the thickness of normal continental crust. Studies of electrical resistivity deduced from magnetotelluric data have detected a layer that appears to contain silicate melt and that stretches for at least 1000 kilometers within the middle crust along the southern margin of the Tibetan Plateau. Granite and rhyolite are types of igneous rock commonly interpreted as products of melting of continental crust because of increases of temperature. Temperature increases also may contribute to the melting of lithosphere dragged down in a subduction zone.

Most magmas only entirely melt for small parts of their histories. More typically, they are mixes of melt and crystals, and sometimes also of gas bubbles. Melt, crystals, and bubbles usually have different densities, and so they can separate as magmas evolve.

As magma cools, minerals typically crystallize from the melt at different temperatures (fractional crystallization). As minerals crystallize, the composition of the residual melt typically changes. If crystals separate from melt, then the residual melt will differ in composition from the parent magma. For instance, a magma of gabbroic composition can produce a residual melt of granitic composition if early formed crystals are separated from the magma. Gabbro may have a liquidus temperature near 1200°C, and derivative granite-composition melt may have a liquidus temperature as low as about 700°C. Incompatible elements are concentrated in the last residues of magma during fractional crystallization and in the first melts produced during partial melting: either process can form the magma that crystallizes to pegmatite, a rock type commonly enriched in incompatible elements. Bowen's reaction series is important for understanding the idealised sequence of fractional crystallisation of a magma.

Magma composition can be determined by processes other than partial melting and fractional crystallization. For instance, magmas commonly interact with rocks they intrude, both by melting those rocks and by reacting with them. Magmas of different compositions can mix with one another. In rare cases, melts can separate into two immiscible melts of contrasting compositions.

There are relatively few minerals that are important in the formation of common igneous rocks, because the magma from which the minerals crystallize is rich in only certain elements: silicon, oxygen, aluminium, sodium, potassium, calcium, iron, and magnesium. These are the elements which combine to form the silicate minerals, which account for over ninety per cent of all igneous rocks. The chemistry of igneous rocks is expressed differently for major and minor elements and for trace elements. Contents of major and minor elements are conventionally expressed as weight per cent oxides (e.g., 51% SiO_2, and 1.50% TiO_2). Abundances of trace elements are conventionally expressed as parts per million by weight (e.g., 420 ppm Ni, and 5.1 ppm Sm). The term "trace element" typically is used for elements present in most rocks at abundances less than 100 ppm or so, but some trace elements may be present in some rocks at abundances exceeding 1000 ppm. The diversity of rock compositions has been defined by a huge mass of analytical data–over 230,000 rock analyses can be accessed on the web through a site sponsored by the U.S. National Science Foundation.

8 Igneous Differentiation

In geology, igneous differentiation is an umbrella term for the various processes by which magmas undergo bulk chemical change during the partial melting process, cooling, emplacement or eruption.

Primary Melts

When a rock melts it melts to form a liquid, the liquid is known as a *primary melt*. Primary melts have not undergone any differentiation and represent the starting composition of a magma. In nature, primary melts are rarely seen. The leucosomes of migmatites are examples of primary melts. Primary melts derived from the mantle are especially important, and are known as *primitive melts* or primitive magmas. By finding the primitive magma composition of a magma series it is possible to model the composition of the rock from which a melt was formed, which is important because we have little direct evidence of the mantle.

Parental Melts

Where it is impossible to find the primitive or primary magma composition, it is often useful to attempt to identify a parental melt. A parental melt is a magma composition from which the observed range of magma chemistries has been derived by the processes of igneous differentiation. It need not be a primitive melt.

For instance, a series of basalt flows are assumed to be related to one another. A composition from which they could reasonably be produced by fractional crystallization is termed a *parental melt*. To prove this, fractional crystallization models would be produced to test the hypothesis that they share a common parental melt.

Cumulate Rocks

Fractional crystallisation and accumulation of crystals formed during the differentiation process of a magmatic event are known as *cumulate rocks*. Identifying whether a rock is a cumulate or not is crucial for understanding if it can be modelled back to a primary melt or a primitive melt, and identifying whether the magma has dropped out cumulate minerals is equally important even for rocks which carry no phenocrysts.

Underlying Causes of Differentiation

The primary cause of change in the composition of a magma is *cooling*, which is an inevitable consequence of the magma being created and migrating from the site of partial melting into an area of lower stress — generally a cooler volume of the crust.

Cooling causes the magma to begin to crystallise minerals from the melt or liquid portion of the magma. Most magmas are a mixture of liquid rock (melt) and minerals (phenocrysts).

Contamination is another cause of magma differentiation. Contamination can be caused by *assimilation* of wall rocks, mixing of two or more magmas or even by replenishment of the magma chamber with fresh, hot magma.

The whole gamut of mechanisms for differentiation has been referred to as the FARM process, which stands for **F**ractional crystallization, **A**ssimilation, **R**eplenishment and **M**agma mixing.

Fractional Crystallization of Igneous Rocks

Fractional crystallization is one of the most important geochemical and physical processes operating within the Earth's crust and mantle.

Fractional crystallization is the removal and segregation from a melt of mineral precipitates, which changes the composition of the melt.

Fractional crystallization in silicate melts (magmas) is a very complex process compared to chemical systems in the laboratory because it is affected by a wide variety of phenomena. Prime amongst these is the composition, temperature and pressure of a magma during its cooling.

The composition of a magma is the primary control on which mineral is crystallized as the melt cools down past the liquidus. For instance in mafic and ultramafic melts, the MgO and SiO_2 contents determine whether forsterite olivine is precipitated or whether enstatite pyroxene is precipitated.

Two magmas of similar composition and temperature at different pressure may crystallize different minerals. An example is high-pressure fractional crystallizaion of granites to produce single-feldspar granite, and low-pressure conditions which produce two-feldspar granites.

The partial pressure of vapour phases in silicate melts is also of prime importance, especially in near-solidus crystallization of granites.

Assimilation

Assimilation is a popular mechanism for explaining the felsification of ultramafic and mafic magmas as they rise through the crust. Assimilation assumes that a hot primitive melt intruding into a cooler, felsic crust will melt the crust and mix with the resulting melt. This then alters the composition of the primitive magma.

Effects of this kind are to be expected, and have been clearly proved in many places. There is, however, a general reluctance to admit that they are of great importance. The nature and succession of the rock species do not as a rule show any relation to the sedimentary or other materials which may be supposed to have been dissolved; and where solution is known to have gone on the products are usually of abnormal character and easily distinguishable from the common rock types.

Replenishment

When a melt undergoes cooling along the liquid line of descent, the results are limited to the production of a homogeneous solid body of intrusive rock, with uniform mineralogy and composition, or a partially differentiated cumulate mass with layers, compositional zones and so on. This behaviour is fairly predictable and easy enough to prove with geochemical investigations. In such cases, a magma chamber will form a close approximation of the ideal Bowen's reaction series. However, most magmatic systems are polyphase events, with several pulses of magmatism. In such a case, the liquid line of descent is interrupted by the injection of a fresh batch of hot, undifferentiated magma. This can cause extreme fractional crystallisation because of three main effects:

- Additional heat provides additional energy to allow more vigorous convection, allows resorption of existing mineral phases back into the melt, and can cause a higher-temperature form of a mineral or other higher-temperature minerals to begin precipitating.
- Fresh magma changes the composition of the melt, changing the chemistry of the phases which are being precipitated. For instance, plagioclase conforms to the liquid line of descent by forming initial anorthite which, if removed, changes the equilibrium mineral composition to oligoclase or albite. Replenishment of the magma can see this trend reversed, so that more anorthite is precipitated atop cumulate layers of albite.

- Fresh magma destabilises minerals which are precipitating as solid solution series or on a eutectic; a change in composition and temperature can cause extremely rapid crystallisation of certain mineral phases which are undergoing a eutectic crystallisation phase.

Magma Mixing

Magma mixing is the process by which two magmas meet, comingle, and form a magma of a composition somewhere between the two end-member magmas.

Magma mixing is a common process in volcanic magma chambers, which are open-system chambers where magmas enter the chamber, undergo some form of assimilation, fractional crystallisation and partial melt extraction (via eruption of lava), and are replenished.

Magma mixing also tends to occur at deeper levels in the crust and is considered one of the primary mechanisms for forming intermediate rocks such as monzonite and andesite. Here, due to heat transfer and increased volatile flux from subduction, the silicic crust melts to form a felsic magma (essentially granitic in composition). These granitic melts are known as an *underplate*. Basaltic primary melts formed in the mantle beneath the crust rise and mingle with the underplate magmas, the result being part-way between basalt and rhyolite; literally an 'intermediate' composition.

Other Mechanisms of Differentiation

Interface entrapment — Convection in a large magma chamber is subject to the interplay of forces generated by thermal convection and the resistance offered by friction, viscosity and drag on the magma offered by the walls of the magma chamber. Often near the margins of a magma chamber which is convecting, cooler and more viscous layers form concentrically from the outside in, defined by breaks in viscosity and temperature. This forms laminar flow, which separates several domains of the magma chamber which can begin to differentiate separately.

Flow banding is the result of a process of fractional crystallization which occurs by convection, if the crystals which are caught in the flow-banded margins are removed from the melt. The friction and viscosity of the magma causes phenocrysts and xenoliths within the magma or lava to slow down near the interface and become trapped in a viscous layer. This can change the composition of the melt in large intrusions, leading to differentiation.

Partial Melt Extraction

With reference to the definitions, above, a magma chamber will tend to cool down and crystallize minerals according to the liquid line of descent. When this occurs, especially in conjunction with zonation and crystal accumulation, and the melt portion is removed, this can change the composition of a magma chamber. In fact, this is basically fractional crystallization, except in this case we are observing a magma chamber which is the remnant left behind from which a daughter melt has been extracted.

If such a magma chamber continues to cool, the minerals it forms and its overall composition will not match a sample liquid line of descent or a parental magma composition.

Typical Behaviours of Magma Chambers

It is worth reiterating that magma chambers are not usually static single entities. The typical magma chamber is formed from a series of injections of melt and magma, and most are also subject to some form of partial melt extraction.

Granite magmas are generally much more viscous than mafic magmas and are usually more homogeneous in composition. This is generally considered to be caused by the viscosity of the magma, which is orders of magnitude higher than mafic magmas. The higher viscosity means that, when melted, a granitic magma will tend to move in a larger concerted mass and be emplaced as a larger mass because it is less fluid and able to move. This is why granites tend to occur as large plutons, and mafic rocks as dikes and sills.

Granites are cooler and are therefore less able to melt and assimilate country rocks. Wholesale contamination is therefore minor and unusual, although mixing of granitic and basaltic melts is not unknown where basalt is injected into granitic magma chambers.

Mafic magmas are more liable to flow, and are therefore more likely to undergo periodic replenishment of a magma chamber. Because they are more fluid, crystal precipitation occurs much more rapidly, resulting in greater changes by fractional crystallisation. Higher temperatures also allow mafic magmas to assimilate wall rocks more readily and therefore contamination is more common and better developed.

Dissolved Gases

All igneous magmas contain dissolved gases (water vapor, carbonic acid, hydrogen sulfide, chlorine, fluorine, boric acid, etc.). Of these water is the principal, and was formerly believed to have percolated downwards from the Earth's surface to the heated rocks below, but is now generally admitted to be an integral part of the magma. Many peculiarities of the structure of the plutonic rocks as contrasted with the lavas may reasonably be accounted for by the operation of these gases, which were unable to escape as the deep-seated masses slowly cooled, while they were promptly given up by the superficial effusions. The acid plutonic or intrusive rocks have never been reproduced by laboratory experiments, and the only successful attempts to obtain, their minerals artificially have been those in which special provision was made for the retention of the 'mineralizing' gases in the crucibles or sealed tubes employed. These gases often do not enter into the composition of the rock-forming minerals, for most of these are free from water, carbonic acid, etc. Hence as crystallization goes on the residual melt must contain an ever-increasing proportion of volatile constituents. It is conceivable that in the final stages the still uncrystallized part of the magma has more resemblance to a solution of mineral matter in superheated steam than to a dry igneous fusion. Quartz, for example, is the last mineral to form in a granite. It bears much of the stamp of the quartz which we know has been deposited from aqueous solution in veins, etc. It is at the same time the most infusible of all the common minerals of rocks. Its late formation shows that in this case it arose at comparatively low temperatures and points clearly to the special importance of the gases of the magma as determining the sequence of crystallization.

When solidification is nearly complete the gases can no longer be retained in the rock and make their escape through fissures towards the surface. They are powerful agents in attacking the minerals of the rocks which they traverse, and instances of their operation are found in the kaolinization of granites, tourmalinization and formation of greisen, deposition of quartz veins, and the group of changes known as propylitization. These 'pneumatolytic' processes are of the first importance in the genesis of many ore deposits. They are a real part of the history of the magma itself and constitute the terminal phases of the volcanic sequence.

Quantifying Igneous Differentiation

There are several methods of directly measuring and quantifying igneous differentiation processes.

Whole rock geochemistry of representative samples, to track changes and evolution of the magma systems.

Using the above, calculating normative mineralogy and investigating trends.

- Trace element geochemistry
- Isotope geochemistry
- Investigating the contamination of magma systems by wall rock assimilation using radiogenic isotopes.

In all cases, the primary and most valuable method for identifying magma differentiation processes is mapping the exposed rocks, tracking mineralogical changes within the igneous rocks and describing field relationships and textural evidence for magma differentiation.

9 Basalt

Basalt is a common extrusive volcanic rock. It is usually grey to black and fine-grained due to rapid cooling of lava at the surface of a planet. It may be porphyritic containing larger crystals in a fine matrix, or vesicular, or frothy scoria. Unweathered basalt is black or grey.

On Earth, most basalt magmas have formed by decompression melting of the mantle. Basalt has also formed on Earth's Moon, Mars, Venus, and even on the asteroid Vesta. Source rocks for the partial melts probably include both peridotite and pyroxenite. The crustal portions of oceanic tectonic plates are composed predominantly of basalt, produced from upwelling mantle below ocean ridges.

The term basalt is at times applied to shallow intrusive rocks with a composition typical of basalt, but rocks of this composition with a phaneritic (coarse) groundmass are generally referred to as diabase (also called dolerite) or gabbro.

The word 'Basalt' is derived from Late Latin *basaltes,* misspelling of L. *basanites* 'very hard stone', which was imported from Ancient Greek ßasa??t?? (basanites), from ß?sa??? (basanos, 'touchstone') and originated in Egyptian *bauhun 'slate'.*

Uses

Basalt is used in construction (e.g. as building blocks or in the groundwork), making cobblestones (from columnar basalt) and in making statues. Heating and extruding basalt yields stone wool, an excellent thermal insulator.

Types

- Tholeiitic basalt is relatively poor in silica and poor in sodium. Included in this category are most basalts of the ocean floor, most large oceanic islands, and continental flood basalts such as the Columbia River Plateau.
- *MORB* (Mid Ocean Ridge Basalt), is characteristically low in incompatible elements. MORB is commonly erupted only at ocean ridges. MORB itself has been subdivided into varieties such as *NMORB* and *EMORB* (slightly more enriched in incompatible elements).
- *High alumina basalt* may be silica-undersaturated or -oversaturated. It has greater than 17 per cent alumina (Al_2O_3) and is intermediate in composition between tholeiite and alkali basalt; the relatively alumina-rich composition is based on rocks without phenocrysts of plagioclase.
- Alkali basalt is relatively poor in silica and rich in sodium. It is silica-undersaturated and may contain feldspathoids, alkali feldspar and phlogopite.
- Boninite is a high-magnesium form of basalt that is erupted generally in back-arc basins, distinguished by its low titanium content and trace element composition.

The mineralogy of basalt is characterized by a preponderance of calcic plagioclase feldspar and pyroxene. Olivine can also be a significant constituent. Accessory minerals present in relatively minor amounts include iron oxides and iron-titanium oxides, such as magnetite, ulvospinel, and ilmenite. Because of the presence of such oxide minerals, basalt can acquire strong magnetic signatures as it cools, and paleomagnetic studies have made extensive use of basalt.

In tholeiitic basalt, pyroxene (augite and orthopyroxene or pigeonite) and calcium-rich plagioclase are common phenocryst minerals. Olivine may also be a phenocryst, and when present, may have rims of pigeonite. The groundmass contains interstitial quartz or tridymite or cristobalite. *Olivine tholeiite* has augite and orthopyroxene or pigeonite with abundant olivine, but olivine may have rims of pyroxene and is unlikely to be present in the groundmass.

Alkali basalts typically have mineral assemblages that lack orthopyroxene but contain olivine. Feldspar phenocrysts typically are labradorite to andesine in composition. Augite is rich in titanium compared to augite in tholeiitic basalt. Minerals such as alkali feldspar, leucite, nepheline, sodalite, phlogopite mica, and apatite may be present in the groundmass.

Basalt has high liquidus and solidus temperatures—values at the Earth's surface are near or above 1200° C (liquidus) and near or below 1000° C (solidus); these values are higher than those of other common igneous rocks.

The majority of tholeiites are formed at approximately 50-100 km depth within the mantle. Many alkali basalts may be formed at greater depths, perhaps as deep as 150-200 km. The origin of high-alumina basalt continues to be controversial, with interpretations that it is a primary melt and that instead it is derived from other basalt types.

Relative to most common igneous rocks basalt compositions are rich in MgO and CaO and low in SiO_2 and the alkali oxides, i.e., $Na_2O + K_2O$, consistent with the TAS classification.

Basalt generally has a composition of 45-55 wt per cent SiO_2, 2-6 wt per cent total alkalis, 0.5-2.0 wt per cent TiO_2, 5-14 wt per cent FeO and 14 wt per cent or more Al_2O_3.

Contents of CaO are commonly near 10 wt per cent, those of MgO commonly in the range 5 to 12 wt per cent.

High alumina basalts have aluminium contents of 17-19 wt per cent Al_2O_3; boninites have magnesium contents of up to 15 per cent MgO. Rare feldspathoid-rich mafic rocks, akin to alkali basalts, may have $Na_2O + K_2O$ contents of 12 per cent or more.

MORB basalts and their intrusive equivalents, gabbros, are the characteristic igneous rocks formed at mid-ocean ridges. They are tholeiites particularly low in total alkalis and in incompatible trace elements, and they have relatively flat REE patterns normalized to mantle or chondrite values. In contrast, alkali basalts have normalized patterns highly enriched in the light REE, and with greater abundances of the REE and of other incompatible elements. Because MORB basalt is considered a key to understanding plate tectonics, its compositions have been much studied. Although MORB compositions are distinctive relative to average compositions of basalts erupted in other environments, they are not uniform. For instance, compositions change with position along the Mid-Atlantic ridge, and the compositions also define different ranges in different ocean basins.

Isotope ratios of elements such as strontium, neodymium, lead, hafnium, and osmium in basalts have been much-studied, so as to learn about evolution of the Earth's mantle. Isotopic ratios of noble gases, such as $^3He/^4He$, are also of great value: for instance, ratios for basalts range from 6 to 10 for mid-ocean ridge tholeiite (normalized to atmospheric values), but to 15-24+ for ocean island basalts thought to be derived from mantle plumes.

Morphology and Textures

The shape, structure and texture of a basalt is diagnostic of how and where it erupted – whether into the sea, in an explosive cinder eruption or as creeping pahoehoe lava flows, the classic image of Hawaiian basalt eruptions.

Subaerial Eruptions

Basalt which erupts under open air (that is, subaerially) forms three distinct types of lava or volcanic deposits: scoria, ash or cinder; breccia and lava flows.

Basalt in the tops of subaerial lava flows and cinder cones will often be highly vesiculated, imparting a lightweight 'frothy' texture to the rock. Basaltic cinders are often red, coloured by oxidized iron from weathered iron-rich minerals such as pyroxene.

'A' a types of blocky, cinder and breccia flows of thick, viscous basaltic lava are common in Hawaii. Pahoehoe is a highly fluid, hot form of basalt which tends to form thin aprons of molten lava which fill up hollows and sometimes forms lava lakes. Lava tubes are common features of pahoehoe eruptions.

Basaltic tuff or pyroclastic rocks are rare but not unknown. Usually basalt is too hot and fluid to build up sufficient pressure to form explosive lava eruptions but occasionally this will happen by trapping of the lava within the volcanic throat and build up of volcanic gases. Hawaii's Mauna Loa volcano erupted in this way in the 19th century, as did Mount Tarawera, New Zealand in its violent 1886 eruption.

Maar volcanoes are typical of small basalt tuffs, formed by explosive eruption of basalt through the crust, forming an apron of mixed basalt and wall rock breccia and a fan of basalt tuff further out from the volcano.

Amygdaloidal structure is common in relict vesicles and beautifully crystallized species of zeolites, quartz or calcite are frequently found.

During the cooling of a thick lava flow, contractional joints or fractures form. If a flow cools relatively rapidly, significant contraction forces build up. While a flow can shrink in the vertical dimension without fracturing, it cannot easily accommodate shrinking in the horizontal direction unless cracks form; the extensive fracture network that develops results in the formation of columns. The topology of the lateral shapes of these columns can broadly be classed as a random cellular network. These structures are often erroneously described as being predominantly hexagonal. In reality, the mean number of sides of all the columns in such a structure is indeed six (by geometrical definition), but polygons with three to twelve or more sides can be observed. Note that the size of the columns depends loosely on the rate of cooling; very rapid cooling may result in very small (<1 cm diametre) columns, while slow cooling is more likely to produce large columns.

When basalt erupts underwater or flows into the sea, contact with the water quenches the surface and the lava forms a distinctive *pillow* shape, through which the hot lava breaks to form another pillow. This *pillow* texture is very common in underwater basaltic flows and is diagnostic of an underwater eruption environment when found in ancient rocks. Pillows typically consist of a fine-grained core with a glassy crust and have radial jointing. The size of individual pillows varies from 10 cm up to several metres.

When *pahoehoe* lava enters the sea it usually forms pillow basalts. However when *a'a* enters the ocean it forms a littoral cone, a small cone-shaped accumulation of tuffaceous debris formed when the blocky *a'a* lava enters the water and explodes from built-up steam.

The island of Surtsey in the Atlantic Ocean is a basalt volcano which breached the ocean surface in 1963. The initial phase of Surtsey's eruption was highly explosive, as the magma was quite wet, causing the rock to be blown apart by the boiling steam to form a tuff and cinder cone. This has subsequently moved to a typical pahoehoe type behaviour.

Volcanic glass may be present, particularly as rinds on rapidly chilled surfaces of lava flows, and is commonly (but not exclusively) associated with underwater eruptions.

The common corrosion features of underwater volcanic basalt suggest that microbial activity may play a significant role in the chemical exchange between basaltic rocks and seawater. The significant amounts of reduced iron, Fe(II), and manganese, Mn(II), present in basaltic rocks provide potential energy sources for bacteria. Recent research has shown that some Fe(II)-oxidizing bacteria cultured from iron-sulfide surfaces are also able to grow with basaltic rock as a source of Fe(II). In recent work at Loihi Seamount, Fe- and Mn-oxidizing bacteria have been cultured from weathered basalts. The impact of bacteria on altering the chemical composition of basaltic glass (and thus, the oceanic crust) and seawater suggest that these interactions may lead to an application of hydrothermal vents to the origin of life.

Basalt is one of the most common rock types in the world. Basalt is the rock most typical of large igneous provinces. The largest occurrences of basalt are in the ocean floor that is almost completely made up by basalt. Above sea level basalt is common in hotspot islands and around volcanic arcs, specially those on thin crust. However, the largest volumes of basalt on land correspond to continental flood basalts. Continental flood basalts are known to exist in the Deccan Traps in India, the Chilcotin Group in British Columbia, Canada, the Paraná Traps in Brazil, the Siberian Traps in Russia, the Karoo flood basalt province in South Africa, the Columbia River Plateau of Washington and Oregon.

Many archipelagoes and island nations have an overwhelming majority of its bedrock made up by basalt due to being above hotspots, for example, Iceland and Hawaii.

Ancient Precambrian basalts are usually only found in fold and thrust belts, and are often heavily metamorphosed. These are known as greenstone belts, because low-grade metamorphism of basalt produces chlorite, actinolite, epidote and other green minerals.

Lunar and Martian Basalt

The dark areas visible on Earth's moon, the lunar maria, are plains of flood basaltic lava flows. These rocks were sampled by the manned American Apollo programme, the robotic Russian Luna programme, and are represented among the lunar meteorites.

Lunar basalts differ from their terrestrial counterparts principally in their high iron contents, which typically range from about 17 to 22 wt per cent FeO. They also possess a stunning range of titanium concentrations (present in the mineral ilmenite), ranging from less than 1 wt per cent TiO_2, to about 13 wt. per cent. Traditionally, lunar basalts have been classified according to their titanium content, with classes being named high-Ti, low-Ti, and very-low-Ti. Nevertheless, global geochemical maps of titanium obtained from the Clementine mission demonstrate that the lunar maria possesses a continuum of titanium concentrations, and that the highest concentrations are the least abundant.

Lunar basalts show exotic textures and mineralogy, particularly shock metamorphism, lack of the oxidation typical of terrestrial basalts, and a complete lack of hydration. While most of the Moon's basalts erupted between about 3 and 3.5 billion years ago, the oldest samples are 4.2 billion years old, and the youngest flows, based on the age dating method of 'crater counting', are estimated to have erupted only 1.2 billion years ago.

Basalt is also a common rock on the surface of Mars, as determined by data sent back from the planet's surface and by Martian meteorites.

ALTERATION OF BASALT

Metamorphism

Basalts are important rocks within metamorphic belts, as they can provide vital information on the conditions of metamorphism within the belt. Various metamorphic facies are named after the mineral assemblages and rock types formed by subjecting basalts to the temperatures and pressures of the metamorphic event. These are:

- Blueschist facies
- Eclogite facies
- Granulite facies
- Greenschist facies
- Zeolite facies

Metamorphosed basalts are important hosts for a variety of hydrothermal ore deposits, including gold deposits, copper deposits, volcanogenic massive sulfide ore deposits and others.

Weathering

Compared to other rocks found on Earth's surface, basalts weather relatively fast. Chemical weathering of basalt minerals release cations such as calcium, sodium and magnesium, which give basaltic areas a strong buffer capacity against acidification. Calcium released by basalts binds up CO_2 from the atmosphere forming $CaCO_3$ acting thus as a CO_2 trap. To this it must be added that the eruption of basalt itself is often associated with the release of large quantities of CO_2 into the atmosphere from volcanic gases.

Carbon sequestration in basalt has been studied as a means of removing carbon dioxide, produced by human industrialization, from the atmosphere. Underwater basalt deposits, scattered in seas around the globe, have the added benefit of the water serving as a barrier to the re-release of CO_2 into the atmosphere.

Andesite

Andesite is an extrusive igneous, volcanic rock, of intermediate composition, with aphanitic to porphyritic texture. In a general sense, it is the intermediate type between basalt and dacite. The mineral assemblage is typically dominated by plagioclase plus pyroxene and/or hornblende. Magnetite, zircon, apatite, ilmenite, biotite, and garnet are common accessory minerals. Alkali feldspar may be present in minor amounts. The quartz-feldspar abundances in andesite and other volcanic rocks are illustrated in QAPF diagrams. Relative alkali and silica contents are illustrated in TAS diagrams.

Classification of andesites may be refined according to the most abundant phenocryst. Example: *hornblende-phyric andesite*, if hornblende is the principal accessory mineral.

Andesite can be considered as the extrusive equivalent of plutonic diorite. Andesites are characteristic of subduction zones, such as the western margin of South America. The name *andesite* is derived from the Andes mountain range.

Andesite is typically formed at convergent plate margins but may occur in other tectonic settings. Intermediate volcanic rocks are created via several processes:

- Hydration melting of peridotite and fractional crystallization.
- Melting of a subducted slab containing sediments.

Magma mixing between felsic rhyolitic and mafic basaltic magmas in an intermediate reservoir prior to emplacement or eruption.

Andesitic magma in island arc regions (i.e., active oceanic margins) comes from the interplay of the subducting plate and the *mantle wedge*, the wedge-shaped region above the subducting plate.

Water in the subducted oceanic lithosphere 'boils off' from the slab by dehydration of hydrous minerals such as amphibole, zeolites, chlorite etc., which are formed in the oceanic lithosphere during hydrothermal circulation at the mid-ocean-ridge. As these minerals are subjected to greenschist or blueschist metamorphism during subduction, they change to more stable, anhydrous forms, releasing water and soluble elements into the overlying wedge of mantle.

The slab itself, or the overlying mantle wedge, may melt. If the slab melts, it may include subducted sediment as well. The water and initial slab melts rise into the mantle wedge, prompting melting of the peridotite to produce basaltic magma with a distinctive enrichment of soluble elements (e.g., K, Ba, and Pb) compared to insoluble elements (e.g., Nb and Ti).

On its way to the surface, the melt stalls and cools, enabling the fractional crystallization of silica poor minerals, thus raising the silica content of the remaining melt and resulting in andesitic magma.

Basaltic magma may also mix with rhyolitic magma. This usually occurs in continental arc areas such as the Andes, where the high geothermal gradient above the subducted plate, and hydrothermal flows within the mantle wedge may create an *underplate* of softened, partially molten continental crust of intermediate or felsic composition. Basaltic magmas intruded into this anomalously hot zone will prompt partial melting of the crust, and may mix with these melts to produce intermediate compositions, typically andesite to trachyte in composition.

Alternatively, the basaltic melt may heat up the overlying arc, prompting partial melting, and may even assimilate sediments, previous volcanic rocks, etcetera, whilst undergoing fractional crystallisation. These rocks are subordinate due to the difficulty in assimilating sufficient cold material by magmas without cooling to a degree that they become immobile.

Ultimately, the resultant composition of andesite and intermediate magmas is the result of fractional crystallisation, assimilation, partial melting and contamination by the subducted slab. These may take considerable effort to resolve the individual components.

In 2009, researchers revealed that andesite was found in two meteorites (numbered GRA 06128 and GRA 06129) that were discovered in the Graves Nunatak Icefield during the US Antarctic Search for Meteorites 2006/2007 field season. This possibly points to a new mechanism to generate andesite crust.

Rhyolite

Rhyolite is an igneous, volcanic (extrusive) rock, of felsic (silica-rich) composition (typically > 69% SiO_2 –. It may have any texture from glassy to aphanitic to porphyritic. The mineral assemblage is usually quartz, alkali feldspar and plagioclase. Biotite and hornblende are common accessory minerals.

Rhyolite can be considered as the extrusive equivalent to the plutonic granite rock, and consequently, outcrops of rhyolite may bear a resemblance to granite. Due to their high content of silica and low iron and magnesium contents, rhyolite melts are highly polymerized and form highly viscous lavas. They can also occur as breccias or in volcanic plugs and dikes. Rhyolites that cool too quickly to grow crystals form a natural glass or vitrophyre, also called obsidian. Slower cooling forms microscopic crystals in the lava and results in textures such as flow foliations, spherulitic, nodular, and lithophysal structures. Some rhyolite is highly vesicular pumice. Many eruptions of rhyolite are highly explosive and the deposits may consist of fallout tephra/tuff or of ignimbrites.

During the second millennium BC, rhyolite was quarried extensively in what is now eastern Pennsylvania in the United States. Among the leading quarries was the Carbaugh Run Rhyolite Quarry Site in Adams County, where as many as fifty small quarry pits are known.

The name rhyolite was introduced into science by the German traveler and geologist Ferdinand von Richthofen after his explorations in the Rocky Mountains in the 1860s.

10 Granite

Granite (pronounced /'græn?t/) is a common and widely occurring type of intrusive, felsic, igneous rock. Granites usually have a medium to coarse grained texture. Occasionally some individual crystals (phenocrysts) are larger than the groundmass in which case the texture is known as porphyritic. A granitic rock with a porphyritic texture is sometimes known as a porphyry. Granites can be pink to gray in colour, depending on their chemistry and mineralogy. By definition, granite has a colour index (i.e. the percentage of the rock made up of dark minerals) of less than 25 per cent. Outcrops of granite tend to form tors, and rounded massifs. Granites sometimes occur in circular depressions surrounded by a range of hills, formed by the metamorphic aureole or hornfels. Granite is usually found in the continental plates of the Earths Crust.

Granite is nearly always massive (lacking internal structures), hard and tough, and therefore it has gained widespread use as a construction stone. The average density of granite is located between 2.65 and 2.75 g/cm^3, its compressive strength usually lies above 200 MPa and its viscosity at standard temperature and pressure is 3-6 • 10^{19} Pa·s.

The word granite comes from the Latin *granum*, a grain, in reference to the coarse-grained structure of such a crystalline rock.

Granitoid is used as a descriptive field term for general, light coloured, coarse-grained igneous rocks for which a more specific name requires petrographic examination.

Granite is classified according to the QAPF diagram for coarse grained plutonic rocks and is named according to the percentage of quartz, alkali feldspar (orthoclase, sanidine, or microcline) and plagioclase feldspar on the A-Q-P half of the diagram. True granite according to modern petrologic convention contains both plagioclase and alkali feldspars. When a granitoid is devoid or nearly devoid of plagioclase the rock is referred to as alkali granite. When a granitoid contains <10 per cent orthoclase it is called tonalite; pyroxene and amphibole are common in tonalite. A granite containing both muscovite and biotite micas is called a binary or *two-mica* granite. Two-mica granites are typically high in potassium and low in plagioclase, and are usually S-type granites or A-type granites. The volcanic equivalent of plutonic granite is rhyolite. Granite has poor primary permeability but strong secondary permeability.

Chemical Composition

A worldwide average of the chemical composition of granite, by weight per cent:

The Stawamus Chief is a granite monolith in British Columbia.

SiO_2	—	72.04	per cent
Al_2O_3	—	14.42	per cent
K_2O	—	4.12	per cent
Na_2O	—	3.69	per cent
CaO	—	1.82	per cent
FeO	—	1.68	per cent

Fe_2O_3	—	1.22	per cent
MgO	—	0.71	per cent
TiO_2	—	0.30	per cent
P_2O_5	—	0.12	per cent
MnO	—	0.05	per cent

Occurrence

Granite is currently known only on Earth where it forms a major part of continental crust. Granite often occurs as relatively small, less than 100 km^2 stock masses (stocks) and in batholiths that are often associated with orogenic mountain ranges. Small dikes of granitic composition called aplites are often associated with the margins of granitic intrusions. In some locations very coarse-grained pegmatite masses occur with granite.

Granite has been intruded into the crust of the Earth during all geologic periods, although much of it is of Precambrian age. Granitic rock is widely distributed throughout the continental crust of the Earth and is the most abundant basement rock that underlies the relatively thin sedimentary veneer of the continents.

Origin

Granite is an igneous rock and is formed from magma. Granitic magma has many potential origins but it must intrude other rocks. Most granite intrusions are emplaced at depth within the crust, usually greater than 1.5 kilometres and up to 50 km depth within thick continental crust. The origin of granite is contentious and has led to varied schemes of classification. Classification schemes are regional and include French, British, and American systems.

Geochemical Origins

Granitoids are a ubiquitous component of the crust. They have crystallized from magmas that have compositions at or near a eutectic point (or a temperature minimum on a cotectic curve). Magmas will evolve to the eutectic because of igneous differentiation, or because they represent low degrees of partial melting. Fractional crystallisation serves to reduce a melt in iron, magnesium, titanium, calcium and sodium, and enrich the melt in potassium and silicon - alkali feldspar (rich in potassium) and quartz (SiO_2), are two of the defining constituents of granite.

This process operates regardless of the origin of the parental magma to the granite, and regardless of its chemistry. However, the composition and origin of the magma which differentiates into granite, leaves certain geochemical and mineral evidence as to what the granite's parental rock was. The final mineralogy, texture and chemical composition of a granite is often distinctive as to its origin. For instance, a granite which is formed from melted sediments may have more alkali feldspar, whereas a granite derived from melted basalt may be richer in plagioclase feldspar. It is on this basis that the modern 'alphabet' classification schemes are based.

Chappell and White Classification System

The letter-based Chappell and White classification system was proposed initially to divide granites into *I-type* granite (or igneous protolith) granite and *S-type* or sedimentary protolith granite. Both of these types of granite are formed by melting of high grade metamorphic rocks, either other granite or intrusive mafic rocks, or buried sediment, respectively.

M-type or mantle derived granite was proposed later, to cover those granites which were clearly sourced from crystallized mafic magmas, generally sourced from the mantle. These are rare, because it is difficult to turn basalt into granite via fractional crystallisation.

A-type or *anorogenic* granites are formed above volcanic 'hot spot' activity and have peculiar mineralogy and geochemistry. These granites are formed by melting of the lower crust under conditions that are usually extremely dry. The rhyolites of the Yellowstone caldera are examples of volcanic equivalents of A-type granite.

An old, and largely discounted theory, *granitization* states that granite is formed in place by extreme metasomatism by fluids bringing in elements e.g. potassium and removing others e.g. calcium to transform the metamorphic rock into a granite. This was supposed to occur across a migrating front. The production of granite by metamorphic heat is difficult, but is observed to occur in certain amphibolite and granulite terrains. In-situ granitisation or melting by metamorphism is difficult to recognise except where leucosome and melanosome textures are present in gneisses. Once a metamorphic rock is melted it is no longer a metamorphic rock and is a magma, so these rocks are seen as a transitional between the two, but are not technically granite as they do not actually intrude into other rocks. In all cases, melting of solid rock requires high temperature, and also water or other volatiles which act as a catalyst by lowering the solidus temperature of the rock.

The ascent and emplacement of large volumes of granite within the upper continental crust is a source of much debate amongst geologists. There is a lack of field evidence for any proposed mechanisms, so hypotheses are predominantly based upon experimental data. There are two major hypotheses for the ascent of magma through the crust:

- Stokes Diapir
- Fracture Propagation

Of these two mechanisms, Stokes diapir was favoured for many years in the absence of a reasonable alternative. The basic idea is that magma will rise through the crust as a single mass through buoyancy. As it rises it heats the wall rocks, causing them to behave as a power-law fluid and thus flow around the pluton allowing it to pass rapidly and without major heat loss. This is entirely feasible in the warm, ductile lower crust where rocks are easily deformed, but runs into problems in the upper crust which is far colder and more brittle. Rocks there do not deform so easily: for magma to rise as a pluton it would expend far too much energy in heating wall rocks, thus cooling and solidifying before reaching higher levels within the crust.

Nowadays fracture propagation is the mechanism preferred by many geologists as it largely eliminates the major problems of moving a huge mass of magma through cold brittle crust. Magma rises instead in small channels along self-propagating dykes which form along new or pre-existing fault systems and networks of active shear zones. As these narrow conduits open, the first magma to enter solidifies and provides a form of insulation for later magma.

Granitic magma must make room for itself or be intruded into other rocks in order to form an intrusion, and several mechanisms have been proposed to explain how large batholiths have been emplaced:

- Stoping, where the granite cracks the wall rocks and pushes upwards as it removes blocks of the overlying crust.
- Assimilation, where the granite melts its way up into the crust and removes overlying material in this way.
- Inflation, where the granite body inflates under pressure and is injected into position.

Most geologists today accept that a combination of these phenomena can be used to explain granite intrusions, and that not all granites can be explained entirely by one or another mechanism.

Natural Radiation

Granite is a natural source of radiation, like most natural stones. However, some granites have been reported to have higher radioactivity thereby raising some concerns about their safety.

Some granites contain around 10 to 20 parts per million of uranium. By contrast, more mafic rocks such as tonalite, gabbro or diorite have 1 to 5 ppm uranium, and limestones and sedimentary rocks usually have equally low amounts. Many large granite plutons are the sources for palaeochannel-hosted or roll front uranium ore deposits, where the uranium washes into the sediments from the granite uplands and associated, often highly radioactive, pegmatites. Granite could be considered a potential natural radiological hazard as, for instance, villages located over granite may be susceptible to higher doses of radiation than other communities. Cellars and basements sunk into soils over granite can become a trap for radon gas, which is formed by the decay of uranium. Radon can also be introduced into houses by wells drilled into granite. Radon gas poses significant health concerns, and is the #2 cause of lung cancer in the US behind smoking.

There is some concern that materials sold as granite countertops or as building material may be hazardous to health. One expert, Dr. Dan Steck of St. Johns University, has stated that approximately 5 per cent of all granites will be of concern, with the caveat that only a tiny percentage of the tens of thousands of granite slabs have been tested. Various resources from national geological survey organizations are accessible online to assist in assessing the risk factors in granite country and design rules relating, in particular, to preventing accumulation of radon gas in enclosed basements and dwellings.

A study of granite countertops was done (initiated and paid for by the Marble Institute of America) in November 2008 by National Health and Engineering Inc of USA, and found that all of the 39 full size granite slabs that were measured for the study showed radiation levels well below the European Union safety standards (section 4.1.1.1 of the National Health and Engineering study) and radon emission levels well below the average outdoor radon concentrations in the US.

Other researchers and organizations do not agree with the Marble Institute's stated position on granite safety, including AARST (American Association of Radon Scientists and Technicians) and the CRCPD (Conference of Radiation Control Programme Directors, an organization of state radiation protection officials). Both organizations have committees currently setting maximum allowed levels of radiation/radon as well as protocols for measuring radiation/ radon from granite countertops. The European Union regulations will likely serve as the basis for new EPA based regulations for granite building materials in the U.S.

The Red Pyramid of Egypt (c.26th century BC), named for the light crimson hue of its exposed granite surfaces, is the third largest of Egyptian pyramids. Menkaure's Pyramid, likely dating to the same era, was constructed of limestone and granite blocks. The Great Pyramid of Giza (c.2580 BC) contains a huge granite sarcophagus fashioned of "Red Aswan Granite." The mostly ruined Black Pyramid dating from the reign of Amenemhat III once had a polished granite pyramidion or capstone, now on display in the main hall of the Egyptian Museum in Cairo (see Dahshur). Other uses in Ancient Egypt include columns, door lintels, sills, jambs, and wall and floor veneer. How the Egyptians worked the solid granite is still a matter of debate. Dr. Patrick Hunt has postulated that the Egyptians used emery shown to have higher hardness on the Mohs scale.

Many large Hindu temples in southern India, particularly those built by the 11th century king Rajaraja Chola I, were made of granite. There is a large amount of granite in these structures. They are comparable to the Great Pyramid of Giza.

Quarrying granite for the Mormon Temple, Utah Territory, in Little Cottonwood Canyon.

Polished Red Granite Tombstone

Granite was used for cobblestones on the St. Louis riverfront and for the piers of the Eads Bridge (background).

Granite has been extensively used as a dimension stone and as flooring tiles in public and commercial buildings and monuments. Aberdeen in Scotland, which is constructed principally from local granite, is known as 'The Granite City'. Because of its abundance, granite was commonly used to build foundations for homes in New England. The Granite Railway, America's first railroad, was built to haul granite from the quarries in Quincy, Massachusetts, to the Neponset River in the 1820s. With increasing amounts of acid rain in parts of the world, granite has begun to supplant marble as a monument material, since it is much more durable. Polished granite is also a popular choice for kitchen countertops due to its high durability and aesthetic qualities. In building and for countertops, the term 'granite' is often applied to all igneous rocks with large crystals, and not specifically to those with a granitic composition.

Other Uses

Curling stones are traditionally fashioned of Ailsa Craig granite. The first stones were made in the 1750s, the original source being Ailsa Craig in Scotland. Because of the particular rarity of the granite, the best stones can cost as much as US$1,500. Between 60-70 per cent of the stones used today are made from Ailsa Craig granite, although the island is now a wildlife reserve and is no longer used for quarrying.

In some areas granite is used for gravestones and memorials. Granite is a hard stone and requires skill to carve by hand. Modern methods of carving include using computer-controlled rotary bits and sandblasting over a rubber stencil. Leaving the letters, numbers and emblems exposed on the stone, the blaster can create virtually any kind of artwork or epitaph.

Engineering

Engineers have traditionally used polished granite surfaces to establish a plane of reference, since they are relatively impervious and inflexible. Sandblasted concrete with a heavy aggregate content has an appearance similar to rough granite, and is often used as a substitute when use of real granite is impractical. A most unusual use of granite was in the construction of the rails for the Haytor Granite Tramway, Devon, England, in 1820.

Granite is one of the rocks most prized by climbers, for its steepness, soundness, crack systems, and friction. Well-known venues for granite climbing include Yosemite, the Bugaboos, the Mont Blanc massif (and peaks such as the Aiguille du Dru, the Mountains of Mourne, the Aiguille du Midi and the Grandes Jorasses), the Bregaglia, Corsica, parts of the Karakoram (especially the Trango Towers), the Fitzroy Massif, Patagonia, Baffin Island, the Cornish coast and the Cairngorms.

Granite rock climbing is so popular that many of the artificial rock climbing walls found in gyms and theme parks are made to look and feel like granite.

Intrusion

An intrusion is liquid rock that forms under the surface of the earth. Magma from under the surface slowly moves its way up from deep within the earth and moves into any cracks or spaces it can find, sometimes pushing existing country rock out of the way, a process that can take millions of years or more to form. As the rock slowly cools into a solid, the different parts of the magma slowly crystallize into minerals. The more slowly the crystals form, the larger the crystals can get. Volcanic rock, by contrast, cools very quickly on the surface of the earth, and thus, generally have only microscopic crystals, such as in an ash cloud (whose crystals are tiny dust particles). Many mountain ranges, such as the Sierra Nevada in California, are formed mostly by intrusive rock, large granite (or related rock) formations.

Intrusions are one of two ways for igneous rock to form; the other way is extrusive, that is, a volcano eruption or similar event. Technically speaking, an intrusion is any formation of intrusive igneous rock; rock formed from magma that cools and solidifies within the crust of a planet. In contrast, an *extrusion* consists of extrusive rock; rock formed above the surface of the crust.

Intrusions vary widely, from mountain range sized batholiths to thin vein-like fracture fillings of aplite or pegmatite. When exposed by erosion, these cores called batholiths may occupy huge areas of Earth's surface. Large bodies of magma that solidify underground before they reach the surface of the crust are called plutons.

Coarse grained intrusive igneous rocks that form at depth within the earth are called abyssal while those that form near the surface are called hypabyssal. Intrusive structures are often classified according to whether or not they are parallel to the bedding planes or foliation of the country rock: if the intrusion is parallel the body is concordant, otherwise it is discordant.

Intrusions can be classified according to the shape and size of the intrusive body and its relation to the other formations into which it intrudes:

- *Batholith:* a large irregular discordant intrusion.
- *Dike:* a relatively narrow tabular discordant body, often nearly vertical.
- *Laccolith:* concordant body with roughly flat base and convex top, usually with a feeder pipe below.
- *Lopolith:* concordant body with roughly flat top and a shallow convex base, may have a feeder dike or pipe below.
- *Phacolith:* a concordant lens-shaped pluton that typically occupies the crest of an anticline or trough of a syncline.

- *Volcanic pipe or volcanic neck:* tubular roughly vertical body that may have been a feeder vent for a volcano.
- *Sill:* a relatively thin tabular concordant body intruded along bedding planes.
- *Stock:* a smaller irregular discordant intrusion.

Deep-seated intrusions are recognized from the way they have burst through the overlaying strata. Ramifying veins result from filled cracks, and the high temperature involved in this process is evident from the altered adjacent country rock. Since heat dissipates slowly and since the rock is under pressure, crystals form and no vitreous rapidly chilled matter is present. As the intrusions have had time to rest before crystallizing, they are not fluidal. Their contained gases have not been able to escape through the thick layer of strata, beneath which they were injected. Such gases form cavities, which can often be observed in these minerals. Such gases have also resulted in many important modifications in the crystallization of the rock. Because their crystals are of approximately equal size these rocks are said to be granular.

There is typically no distinction between a first generation of large well-shaped crystals and a fine-grained ground-mass. The minerals of each have formed in a definite order, and each has had a period of crystallization that may be very distinct or may have coincided with or overlapped the period of formation of some of the other ingredients. Earlier crystals originated at a time when most of the rock was still liquid and are more or less perfect. Later crystals are less regular in shape because they were compelled to occupy the spaces left between the already-formed crystals. The former case is said to be idiomorphic (or *automorphic*); the latter is xenomorphic. There are also many other characteristics that serve to distinguish the members of these two groups. For example, orthoclase is typically feldspar from granite, while its modifications occur in lavas of similar composition. The same distinction holds for nepheline varieties. Leucite is common in lavas but very rare in plutonic rocks. Muscovite is confined to intrusions. These differences show the influence of the physical conditions under which consolidation takes placc.

Some intrusive rocks solidified in fissures as dikes and intrusive sills at a shallow depth beneath the surface and are called hypabyssal. Those formed at greater depths are called plutonic or *abyssal*. As might be expected, they show structures intermediate between those of extrusive and plutonic rocks. They are very commonly porphyritic, vitreous, and sometimes even vesicular. In fact, many of them are petrologically indistinguishable from lavas of similar composition.

Diorite

Diorite is a grey to dark grey intermediate intrusive igneous rock composed principally of plagioclase feldspar (typically andesine), biotite, hornblende, and/or pyroxene. It may contain small amounts of quartz, microcline and olivine. Zircon, apatite, sphene, magnetite, ilmenite and sulfides occur as accessory minerals. It can also be black or bluish-grey, and frequently has a greenish cast. Varieties deficient in hornblende and other dark minerals are called *leucodiorite*. When olivine and more iron-rich augite are present, the rock grades into ferrodiorite, which is transitional to gabbro. The presence of significant quartz makes the rock type quartz-diorite (>5% quartz) or tonalite (>20% quartz), and if orthoclase (potassium feldspar) is present at greater than ten per cent the rock type grades into monzodiorite or granodiorite. Diorite has a medium grain size texture, occasionally with porphyry.

Diorites may be associated with either granite or gabbro intrusions, into which they may subtly merge. Diorite results from partial melting of a mafic rock above a subduction zone. It is commonly produced in volcanic arcs, and in cordilleran mountain building such as in the Andes Mountains as large batholiths. The extrusive volcanic equivalent rock type is andesite.

Diorite is a relatively rare rock; source localities include Leicestershire; UK (one name for microdiorite - Markfieldite - exists due to the rock being found in the village of Markfield), Sondrio, Italy; Thuringia and Saxony in Germany; Finland; Romania; Northeastern Turkey; central Sweden; Scotland; the Darrans range of New Zealand; the Andes Mountains; the Isle of Guernsey; Basin and Range province and Minnesota in the USA; Idahet in Egypt.

Diorite is an extremely hard rock, making it difficult to carve and work with. It is so hard that ancient civilizations (such as Ancient Egypt) used diorite balls to work granite. Its hardness, however, also allows it to be worked finely and take a high polish, and to provide a durable finished work.

One comparatively frequent use of diorite was for inscription, as it is easier to carve in relief than in three-dimensional statuary. Perhaps the most famous diorite work extant is the Code of Hammurabi, inscribed upon a 2.23m (7ft 4in) pillar of black diorite. The original can be seen today in Paris' Musée de Louvre. The use of diorite in art was most important among very early Middle Eastern civilizations such as Ancient Egypt, Babylonia, Assyria and Sumer. It was so valued in early times that the first great Mesopotamian empire — the Empire of Sargon of Akkad — listed the taking of diorite as a purpose of military expeditions.

Although one can find diorite art from later periods, it became more popular as a structural stone and was frequently used as pavement due to its durability. Diorite was used by both the Inca and Mayan civilizations, but mostly for fortress walls, weaponry, etc. It was especially popular with medieval Islamic builders. In later times, diorite was commonly used as cobblestone; today many diorite cobblestone streets can be found in England, Guernsey and Scotland, and scattered throughout the world in such places as Ecuador and China. Although diorite is rough-textured in nature, its ability to take a polish can be seen in the diorite steps of St. Paul's Cathedral, London, where centuries of foot traffic have polished the steps to a sheen.

Dike

A dike or dyke in geology is a type of sheet intrusion referring to any geologic body that cuts *discordantly* across.

- planar wall rock structures, such as bedding or foliation
- massive rock formations, like igneous/magmatic intrusions and salt diapirs.

Dikes can therefore be either intrusive or sedimentary in origin.

An intrusive dike is an igneous body with a very high aspect ratio, which means that its thickness is usually much smaller than the other two dimensions. Thickness can vary from sub-centimeter scale to many meters, and the lateral dimensions can extend over many kilometres. A dike is an intrusion into an opening cross-cutting fissure, shouldering aside other pre-existing layers or bodies of rock; this implies that a dike is always younger than the rocks that contain it. Dikes are usually high angle to near vertical in orientation, but subsequent tectonic deformation may rotate the sequence of strata through which the dike propagates so that the latter becomes horizontal. Near horizontal, or conformable intrusions, along bedding planes between strata are called intrusive sills.

Sometimes dikes appear as swarms, consisting of several to hundreds of dikes emplaced more or less contemporaneously during a single intrusive event. The world's largest dike swarm is the Mackenzie dike swarm in the Northwest Territories, Canada.

Dikes often form as either radial or concentric swarms around plutonic intrusives, volcanic necks or feeder vents in volcanic cones. The latter are known as ring dikes.

Dikes can vary in texture and their composition can range from diabase or basaltic to granitic or rhyolitic, but on a global perspective the basaltic composition prevails, manifesting ascent of vast volumes of mantle-derived magmas through fractured lithosphere throughout Earth history. Pegmatite dikes are extremely coarse crystalline granitic rocks often associated with late-stage granite intrusions or metamorphic segregations. Aplite dikes are fine grained or sugary textured intrusives of granitic composition.

Sedimentary dikes or clastic dikes are vertical bodies of sedimentary rock that cut off other rock layers. They can form in two ways:

- When a shallow unconsolidated sediment is composed of alternating coarse grained and impermeable clay layers the fluid pressure inside the coarser layers may reach a critical value due to lithostatic overburden. Driven by the fluid pressure the sediment breaks through overlying layers and forms a dike.
- When a soil is under permafrost conditions the pore water is totally frozen. When cracks are formed in such rocks, they may fill up with sediments that fall in from above. The result is a vertical body of sediment that cuts through horizontal layers: a dike.

11 Rock Microstructure

Rock microstructure includes the texture of a rock and the small scale rock structures. The words 'texture' and 'microstructure' are interchangeable, with the latter preferred in modern geological literature. However, texture is still acceptable because it is a useful means of identifying the origin of rocks, how they formed, and their appearance.

Textures are *penetrative fabrics* of rocks; they occur throughout the entirety of the rock mass on a microscopic, hand specimen and often on an outcrop scale. This is similar in many ways to foliations, except a texture does not necessarily carry structural information in terms of deformation events and orientation information. Structures occur on hand-specimen scale and above.

Microstructure analysis describes the textural features of the rock, and can provide information on the conditions of formation, petrogenesis, and subsequent deformation, folding or alteration events.

Sedimentary Microstructures

Description of sedimentary rock microstructure aims to provide information on the conditions of deposition of the sediment, the paleo-environment, and the provenance of the sedimentary material.

Methods involve description of clast size, sorting, composition, rounding or angularity, sphericity and description of the matrix. Sedimentary microstructures, specifically, may include microscopic analogs of larger sedimentary structural features such as cross-bedding, syn-sedimentary faults, sediment slumping, cross-stratification, etc.

Maturity

The maturity of a sediment is related not only to the sorting (mean grain size and deviations), but also to the fragment sphericity, rounding and composition. Quartz-only sands are more mature than arkose or greywacke.

Fragment Shape

Fragment shape gives information on the length of sediment transport. The more rounded the clasts, the more water-worn they are. Particle shape includes form and rounding. Form indicates whether a grain is more equant (round, spherical) or platy (flat, disc-like, oblate); as well as sphericity.

Roundness

Roundness refers to the degree of sharpness of the corners and edges of a grain. The surface texture of grains may be polished, frosted, or marked by small pits and scratches. This information can usually be seen best under a binocular microscope, not in a thin section.

Composition

Composition of the clasts can give clues as to the derivation of a rock's sediments. For instance, volcanic fragments, fragments of cherts, well-rounded sands all imply different sources.

Matrix and Cement

The matrix of a sedimentary rock and the mineral cement (if any) holding it together are all diagnostic.

Diagenetic Features

Usually diagenesis results in a weak bedding-plane foliation. Other effects can include flattening of grains, pressure dissolution and sub-grain deformation. Mineralogical changes may include zeolite or other authigenic minerals forming in low-grade metamorphic conditions.

Sorting

Sorting is used to describe the uniformity of grain sizes within a sedimentary rock. Understanding sorting is critical to making inferences on the degree of maturity and length of transport of a sediment. Sorting can be expressed mathematically by the standard deviation of the grain-size frequency curve of a sediment sample, expressed as values of f (phi). Values range from <0.35f (very well sorted) to >4.00f (extremely poorly sorted).

Metamorphic Microstructure

The study of metamorphic rock microstructures aims to determine the timing, sequence and conditions of deformations, mineral growth and overprinting of subsequent deformation events.

Metamorphic microstructures include textures formed by the development of foliation and overprinting of foliations causing crenulations. The relationship of porphyroblasts to the foliations and to other porphyroblasts can provide information on the order of formation of metamorphic assemblages or facies of minerals.

Shear textures are particularly suited to analysis by microstructural investigations, especially in mylonites and other highly disturbed and deformed rocks.

Foliations and Crenulations

On the thin section and hand specimen scale a metamorphic rock may manifest a linear penetrative fabric called a foliation or a cleavage. Several foliations may be present in a rock, giving rise to a crenulation.

Identifying a foliation and its orientation is the first step in analysis of foliated metamorphic rocks. Gaining information on when the foliation formed is essential to reconstructing a P-T-t (pressure, temperature, time) path for a rock, as the relationship of a foliation to porphyroblasts is diagnostic of when the foliation formed, and the P-T conditions which existed at that time.

Ductile Shear Microstructures

Very distinctive textures form as a consequence of ductile shear. The microstructures of ductile shear zones are S-planes, C-planes and C' planes. S-planes or *sissalement* planes are parallel with the shear direction and are generally defined by micas or platy minerals. Define the flattened long-axis of the strain ellipse. C-planes or *cissalement* planes form oblique to the shear plane. The angle between the C and S planes is always acute, and defines the shear sense. Generally, the lower the C-S angle the greater the strain. The C' planes are rarely observed except in ultradeformed mylonites, and form nearly perpendicular to the S-plane.

Other microstructures which can give sense of shear include:

- sigmoidal veins
- mica fish
- rotated porphyroblasts.

Igneous Microstructure

Analysis of igneous rock microstructure may complement descriptions on the hand specimen and outcrop scale. This is especially vital for describing phenocrysts and fragmental textures of tuffs, as often relationships between magma and phenocryst morphology are critical for analysing cooling, fractional crystallization and emplacement.

Analysis of intrusive rock microstructures can provide information on source and genesis, including contamination of igneous rocks by wall rocks and identifying crystals which may have been accumulated or dropped out of the melt. This is especially critical for komatiite lavas and ultramafic intrusive rocks.

General Principles of Igneous Microstructure

Igneous microstructure is a combination of cooling rate, nucleation rate, eruption (if a lava), magma composition and its relationships to what minerals will nucleate, as well as physical effects of wall rocks, contamination and especially vapour.

Grain Texture

According to the texture of the grains, igneous rocks may be classified as:

- *pegmatitic:* very large crystals
- *phaneritic:* rocks contain minerals with crystals visible to the unaided eye, commonly intrusive
- *aphanitic:* rapid cooling, crystal nucleation and growth is stunted, forming a uniform, fine grained rock
- *porphyritic:* containing phenocrysts in a fine groundmass
- *vesicular:* contains voids caused by trapped gas while cooling
- *vitreous:* glassy or hyaline without crystals
- *pyroclastic:* rock contain fragments of crystals, phenocrysts and rock fragments
- *equigranular:* rock crystals are all the same size

Crystal Shapes

Crystal shape is also an important factor in the texture of an igneous rock. Crystals may be euhedral, subeuhedral or anhedral:

- *Euhedral* or *automorphic*, if the crystallographic shape is preserved.
- *Subeuhedral* or *Subhedral*, if only part is preserved.
- *Anhedral* or xenomorphic, if the crystals present no recognizable crystallographic forms.

Rocks composed entirely of euhedral crystals are termed *panidiomorphic*, and rocks composed entirely of subhedral crystals are termed *subidiomorphic*.

Porphyritic Structure

Porphyritic structure is caused by the nucleation of crystal sites and the growth of crystals in a liquid magma. Often a magma can only grow one mineral at a time especially if it is cooling slowly. This is why most igneous rocks have only one type of phenocryst mineral. Rhythmic cumulate layers in ultramafic intrusions are a result of uninterrupted slow cooling.

When a rock cools too quickly the liquid freezes into a solid glass, or crystalline groundmass. Often vapor loss from a magma chamber will cause a porphyritic texture.

Embayments or 'corroded' margins to phenocrysts infer that they were being resorbed by the magma and may imply addition of fresh, hotter magma. Ostwald ripening is also used to explain some porphyritic igneous textures, especially orthoclase megacrystic granites.

Phenocryst Shape: Implications

A crystal growing in a magma adopts a habit (see crystallography) which best reflects its environment and cooling rate. The usual phenocryst habit is the ones commonly observed. This may imply a 'normal' cooling rate.

Abnormal cooling rates occur in supercooled magmas, particularly komatiite lavas. Here, low nucleation rates due to superfluidity prevent nucleation until the liquid is well below the mineral growth curve. Growth then occurs at extreme rates, favoring slender, long crystals. Additionally, at crystal vertices and terminations, spikes and skeletal shapes may form because nucleation favors crystal edges. Spinifex or dendritic texture is an example of this result. Hence, the shape of phenocrysts can provide valuable information on cooling rate and initial magma temperature.

Spherulites

Spherulitic texture is the result of cooling and nucleation of material in a magma which has achieved supersaturation in the crystal component. Thus it is often a subsolidus process in supercooler felsic rocks. Often, two minerals will grow together in the spherulite. Axiolitic texture results from spherulitic growth along fractures in volcanic glass, often from invasion of water.

Graphic and Other Intergrowth Textures

Intergrowths of two or more minerals can form in a variety of ways, and interpretations of the intergrowths can be critical in understanding both magmatic and cooling histories of igneous rocks. A few of the many important textures are presented here as examples.

Graphic, micrographic texture, and granophyric textures are examples of intergrowths formed during magmatic crystallization. They are angular intergrowths of quartz and alkali feldspar. When well-developed, the intergrowths may resemble ancient cuneiform writing, hence the name. These intergrowths are typical of pegmatite and granophyre, and they have been interpreted as documenting simultaneous crystallization of the intergrown minerals in the presence of a silicate melt together with a water-rich phase.

Intergrowths that form by exsolution are aids in interpreting cooling histories of rocks. Perthite is an intergrowth of K-feldspar with albite feldspar, formed by exsolution from an alkali feldspar of intermediate composition: the coarseness of perthitic intergrowths is related to cooling rate. Perthite is typical of many granites. Myrmekite is a microscopic, vermicular (worm-like) intergrowth of quartz and sodium-rich plagioclase common in granite; myrmekite may form as alkali feldspar breaks down by exsolution and silicon is transported by fluids in cooling rocks.

Iron-titanium oxides are extremely important, as they carry the predominant magnetic signatures of many rocks, and so they have played a major role in our understanding of plate tectonics. These oxides commonly have complex textures related both to exsolution and oxidation. For instance, ulvospinel in igneous rocks such as basalt and gabbro commonly oxidizes during subsolidus cooling to produce regular intergrowths of magnetite and ilmenite. The process can determine what magnetic record is inherited by the rock.

Gabbro

Gabbro refers to a large group of dark, coarse-grained, intrusive mafic igneous rocks chemically equivalent to basalt. The rocks are plutonic, formed when molten magma is trapped beneath the Earth's surface and cools into a crystalline mass.

The vast majority of the Earth's surface is underlain by gabbro within the oceanic crust, produced by basalt magmatism at mid-ocean ridges.

Gabbro is dense, greenish or dark-coloured and contains pyroxene, plagioclase, amphibole, and olivine (olivine gabbro when olivine is present in a large amount).

The pyroxene is mostly clinopyroxene; small amounts of orthopyroxene may be present. If the amount of orthopyroxene is substantially greater than the amount of clinopyroxene, the rock is then a norite. Quartz gabbros are also known to occur and are probably derived from magma that was over-saturated with silica. Essexites represent gabbros whose parent magma was under-saturated with silica, resulting in the formation of the feldspathoid mineral nepheline. (Silica saturation of a rock can be evaluated by normative mineralogy). Gabbros contain minor amounts, typically a few percent, of iron-titanium oxides such as magnetite, ilmenite, and ulvospinel.

Gabbro is generally coarse grained, with crystals in the size range of 1 mm or greater. Finer grained equivalents of gabbro are called diabase, although the vernacular term *microgabbro* is often used when extra descriptiveness is desired. Gabbro may be extremely coarse grained to pegmatitic, and some pyroxene-plagioclase cumulates are essentially coarse grained gabbro, although these may exhibit acicular crystal habits.

Gabbro is usually equigranular in texture, although it may be porphyritic at times, especially when plagioclase oikocrysts have grown earlier than the groundmass minerals.

Distribution

Gabbro can be formed as a massive, uniform intrusion via in-situ crystallisation of pyroxene and plagioclase, or as part of a layered intrusion as a cumulate formed by settling of pyroxene and plagioclase. Cumulate gabbros are more properly termed pyroxene-plagioclase orthocumulate.

Gabbro is an essential part of the oceanic crust, and can be found in many ophiolite complexes as parts of zones III and IV (sheeted dyke zone to massive gabbro zone). Long belts of gabbroic intrusions are typically formed at proto-rift zones and around ancient rift zone margins, intruding into the rift flanks. Mantle plume hypotheses may rely on identifying mafic and ultramafic intrusions and coeval basalt volcanism.

Uses

Gabbro often contains valuable amounts of chromium, nickel, cobalt, gold, silver, platinum, and copper sulfides.

Ocellar varieties of gabbro can be used as ornamental facing stones, paving stones and it is also known by the trade name of 'black granite', which is a popular type of graveyard headstone used in funerary rites. It is also used in kitchens and their countertops, also under the misnomer of 'black granite'.

12 Crystallization

Crystallization is the (natural or artificial) process of formation of solid crystals precipitating from a solution, melt or more rarely deposited directly from a gas. Crystallization is also a chemical solid-liquid separation technique, in which mass transfer of a solute from the liquid solution to a pure solid crystalline phase occurs.

The crystallization process consists of two major events, *nucleation* and *crystal growth. Nucleation* is the step where the solute molecules dispersed in the solvent start to gather into clusters, on the nanometer scale (elevating solute concentration in a small region), that becomes stable under the current operating conditions. These stable clusters constitute the nuclei. However when the clusters are not stable, they redissolve. Therefore, the clusters need to reach a critical size in order to become stable nuclei. Such critical size is dictated by the operating conditions (temperature, supersaturation, etc.). It is at the stage of nucleation that the atoms arrange in a defined and periodic manner that defines the crystal structure — note that 'crystal structure' is a special term that refers to the relative arrangement of the atoms, not the macroscopic properties of the crystal (size and shape), although those are a result of the internal crystal structure.

The *crystal growth* is the subsequent growth of the nuclei that succeed in achieving the critical cluster size. Nucleation and growth continue to occur simultaneously while the supersaturation exists. Supersaturation is the driving force of the crystallization, hence the rate of nucleation and growth is driven by the existing supersaturation in the solution. Depending upon the conditions, either nucleation or growth may be predominant over the other, and as a result, crystals with different sizes and shapes are obtained (control of crystal size and shape constitutes one of the main challenges in industrial manufacturing, such as for pharmaceuticals). Once the supersaturation is exhausted, the solid-liquid system reaches equilibrium and the crystallization is complete, unless the operating conditions are modified from equilibrium so as to supersaturate the solution again.

Many compounds have the ability to crystallize with different crystal structures, a phenomenon called polymorphism. Each polymorph is in fact a different thermodynamic solid state and crystal polymorphs of the same compound exhibit different physical properties, such as dissolution rate, shape (angles between facets and facet growth rates), melting point, etc. For this reason, polymorphism is of major importance in industrial manufacture of crystalline products.

Crystallization in Nature

Snow flakes are a very well known example, where subtle differences in *crystal growth* conditions result in different geometries.

There are many examples of natural process that involve crystallization.

Geological time scale process examples include:

- Natural (mineral) crystal formation
- Stalactite/ stalagmite, rings formation.

Usual time scale process examples include:

- Snow flakes formation
- Honey crystallization (nearly all types of honey crystallize).

Artificial Methods

For crystallization (see also recrystallization) to occur from a solution it must be supersaturated. This means that the solution has to contain more solute entities (molecules or ions) dissolved than it would contain under the equilibrium (saturated solution). This can be achieved by various methods, with:

1. solution cooling;
2. addition of a second solvent to reduce the solubility of the solute (technique known as antisolvent or drown-out);
3. chemical reaction; and
4. change in pH being the most common methods used in industrial practice.

Other methods, such as solvent evaporation, can also be used. The spherical crystallization has some advantages (flowability and bioavailability) for the formulation of pharmaceutical drugs

Applications

There are two major groups of applications for the *artificial crystallization* process: *crystal production* and purification.

Crystal Production

From a material industry perspective:

- *Macroscopic crystal* production: for supply the demand of natural-like crystals with methods that "accelerate time-scale" for massive production and/or perfection;

- *Ionic crystal* production;
- *Covalent crystal* production.

Tiny size crystals: *Powder, sand and smaller sizes*: using methods for powder and controlled (nanotechnology fruits) forms.

- *Mass-production*: on chemical industry, like salt-powder production.
- *Sample production*: small production of tiny crystals for material characterization. Controlled recrystallization is an important method to supply unusual crystals, that are needed to reveal the molecular structure and nuclear forces inside a typical molecule of a crystal. Many techniques, like X-ray crystallography and NMR spectroscopy, are widely used in chemistry and biochemistry to determine the structures of an immense variety of molecules, including inorganic compounds and bio-macromolecules.
- Thin film production.

Massive production examples:

- 'Powder salt for food' industry
- Silicon crystal wafer production
- Production of sucrose from sugar beet, where the sucrose is crystallized out from an aqueous solution.

Purification

Used to improve (obtaining very pure substance) and/ or verify their purity.

Crystallization separates a product from a liquid feedstream, often in extremely pure form, by cooling the feedstream or adding precipitants which lower the solubility of the desired product so that it forms crystals.

Well formed crystals are expected to be pure because each molecule or ion must fit perfectly into the lattice as it leaves the solution. Impurities would normally not fit as well in the lattice, and thus remain in solution preferentially. Hence, molecular recognition is the principle of purification in crystallization. However, there are instances when impurities incorporate into the lattice, hence, decreasing the level of purity of the final crystal product. Also, in some cases, the solvent may incorporate into the lattice forming a *solvate*. In addition, the solvent may be 'trapped' (in liquid state) within the crystal formed, and this phenomenon is known as *inclusion*.

Thermodynamic View

Low-temperature SEM magnification series for a snow crystal. The crystals are captured, stored, and sputter coated with platinum at cryo-temperatures for imaging.

The nature of a crystallization process is governed by both thermodynamic and kinetic factors, which can make it highly variable and difficult to control. Factors such as impurity level, mixing regime, vessel design, and cooling profile can have a major impact on the size, number, and shape of crystals produced.

Now put yourself in the place of a molecule within a pure and *perfect crystal*, being heated by an external source. At some sharply defined temperature, a bell rings, you must leave your neighbours, and the complicated architecture of the crystal collapses to that of a liquid. Textbook thermodynamics says that melting occurs because the entropy, S, gain in your system by spatial randomization of the molecules has overcome the enthalpy, H, loss due to breaking the crystal packing forces:

$$T(S_{liquid} - S_{solid}) > H_{liquid} - H_{solid}$$

$$G_{liquid} < G_{solid}$$

This rule suffers no exceptions when the temperature is rising. By the same token, on cooling the melt, at the very same temperature the bell should ring again, and molecules should click back into the very same crystalline form. The entropy decrease due to the ordering of molecules within the system is overcompensated by the thermal randomization of the surroundings, due to the release of the heat of fusion; the entropy of the universe increases.

But liquids that behave in this way on cooling are the exception rather than the rule; in spite of the second principle of thermodynamics, crystallization usually occurs at lower temperatures (supercooling). This can only mean that a crystal is more easily destroyed than it is formed. Similarly, it is usually much easier to dissolve a perfect crystal in a solvent than to grow again a good crystal from the resulting solution. The nucleation and growth of a crystal are under kinetic, rather than thermodynamic, control.

Equipment for Crystallization

1. *Tank crystallizers:* Tank crystallization is an old method still used in some specialized cases. Saturated solutions, in tank crystallization, are allowed to cool in open tanks. After a period of time the mother liquid is drained and the crystals removed. Nucleation and size of crystals are difficult to control. Typically, labour costs are very high.
2. *Scraped surface crystallizers:* One type of scraped surface crystallizer is the Swenson-Walker crystallizer, which consists of an open trough 0.6 m wide with a semicircular bottom having a cooling jacket outside. A slow-speed spiral agitator rotates and suspends the growing crystals on turning. The blades pass close to the wall and break off any deposits of crystals on the cooled wall. The product generally has a somewhat wide crystal-size distribution.
3. *Double-pipe scraped surface crystallizer:* Also called a *votator*, this type of crystallizer is used in crystallizing ice cream and plasticizing margarine. Cooling water

passes in the annular space. An internal agitator is fitted with spring-loaded scrapers that wipe the wall and provide good heat-transfer coefficients.

4. *Circulating-liquid evaporator-crystallizer:* Also called *Oslo crystallizer.* Here supersaturation is reached by evaporation. The circulating liquid is drawn by the screw pump down inside the tube side of the condensing stream heater. The heated liquid then flows into the vapour space, where flash evaporation occurs, giving some supersaturation.The vapour leaving is condensed. The supersaturated liquid flows down the downflow tube and then up through the bed of fluidized and agitated crystals, which are growing in size. The leaving saturated liquid then goes back as a recycle stream to the heater, where it is joined by the entering fluid. The larger crystals settle out and slurry of crystals and mother liquid is withdrawn as a product.

5. *Circulating-magma vacuum crystallizer:* The magma or suspension of crystals is circulated out of the main body through a circulating pipe by a screw pump. The magma flows though a heater, where its temperature is raised 2-6 K. The heated liquor then mixes with body slurry and boiling occurs at the liquid surface. This causes supersaturation in the swirling liquid near the surface, which deposits in the swirling suspended crystals until they leave again via the circulating pipe. The vapours leave through the top. A steam-jet ejector provides vacuum.

6. *Continuous oscillatory baffled crystallizer* (*COBC*)*:* The COBC is a tubular baffled crystallizer that offers plug flow under laminar flow conditions (low flow rates) with superior heat transfer coefficient, allowing controlled cooling profiles, e.g. linear, parabolic, discontinued, step-wise or any type, to be achieved. This gives much better control over crystal size, morphology and consistent crystal products.

The Surface Pattern on This Pedestal Rock is Honeycomb Weathering, Caused By Salt Crystallization. This Example is at Yehliu, Taiwan

Basalt (An Extrusive Igneous Rock in this Case); Light Coloured Tracks Show the Direction of Lava Flow

Vesicular Basalt at Sunset Crater, Arizona. U.S.
Quarter for Scale

Columnar Jointing in the Basalt of the Giant's Causeway in Northern Ireland

Columnar Jointed Basalt in Turkey

A Sample of Andesite (Dark Groundmass) with Amygdaloidal Vesicules Filled with Zeolite. Diametre of View is 8 cm

Quartz and Alkali Feldspar

The Stawamus Chief is a Granite Monolith in British Columbia

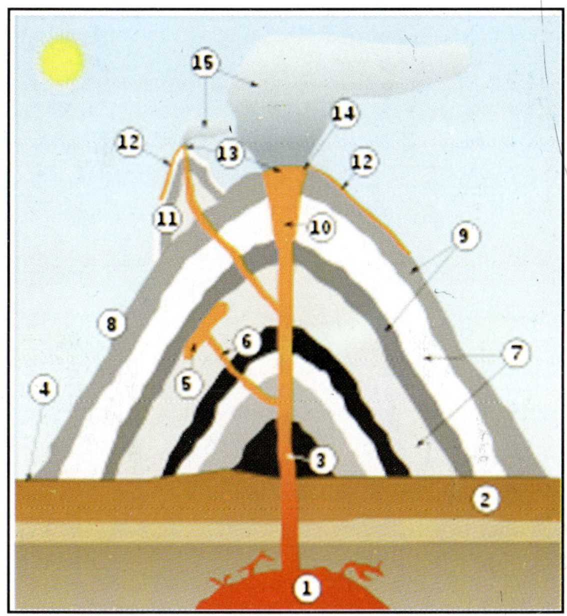

Cross-section Through a Stratovolcano (Vertical Scale is Exaggerated: 1. Large Magma Chamber; 2. Bedrock; 3. Conduit (pipe); 4. Base; 5. Sill; 6. Dike; 7. Layers of Ash Emitted by the Volcano

Pillow Lava (NOAA)

Active Volcano Mount St. Helens Shortly After the Eruption of 18th May 1980

Tavurvur in Papua New Guinea Erupting Peléan

Ash Plume from Mt Cleveland, a Stratovolcano

Fort Rock, An Eroded Tuff Ring in Oregon, USA

Sample of Igneous Gabbro

Sedimentary Sandstone with Iron Oxide Bands

The Permian Through Jurassic stratigraphy of the Colorado Plateau area of southeastern Utah that makes up much of the famous prominent rock formations in protected areas such as Capitol Reef National Park and Canyonlands National Park. From top to bottom: Rounded tan domes of the Navajo Sandstone, layered red Kayenta Formation, cliff-forming, vertically jointed, red Wingate Sandstone, slope-forming, purplish Chinle Formation, layered, lighter-red Moenkopi Formation, and white, layered Cutler Formation sandstone. Picture from Glen Canyon National Recreation Area, Utah

A Rock in Abisko, Sweden Fractured Along Existing Joints Possibly by Frost Weathering or Thermal Stress

A Freshly Broken Rock Shows Differential Chemical Weathering (Probably mostly Oxidation) Progressing inward. This Piece of Standstone was found in Glacial Drift near Angelica, New York

Oxidized Pyrite Cubes

Wadi in Makhtesh Ramon, Israel, Showing Gravity Collapse Erosion on Its Banks

Folded Foliation in a Metamorphic Rock from near Geirangerfjord, Norway

Slate Roof

Limestone in Waitomo District, New Zealand

The Granite Peaks of the Torres del Paine
in the Chilean Patagonia

A *dike* Intrudes into the Country Rock
Baranof Island, Alaska, USA

Diorite

A Small Dike on the Baranof Cross-Island Trail, Alaska

Gabbro Specimen; Rock Creek Canyon Eastern Sierra Nevada, California

Claystone Deposited in Glacial Lake Missoula, Montana, USA. Note Very Fine and Flat Bedding, Common for Distal Lacustrine Deposition

Cross-bedding and Scour in a Fine Sandstone; the Logan Formation (Mississippian) of Jackson County, Ohio

Ripple Marks Formed by a Current in a Sandstone that was Later Titled. Location: Haberge, Bavaria

13 Sedimentary Rock

Sedimentary rock is a type of rock that is formed by sedimentation of material at the Earth's surface and within bodies of water. Sedimentation is the collective name for processes that cause mineral and/or organic particles (detritus) to settle and accumulate or minerals to precipitate from a solution. Particles that form a sedimentary rock by accumulating are called sediment. Before being deposited, sediment was formed by weathering and erosion in a source area, and then transported to the place of deposition by water, wind, mass movement or glaciers which are called agents of denudation.

The sedimentary rock cover of the continents of the Earth's crust is extensive, but the total contribution of sedimentary rocks is estimated to be only five per cent of the total volume of the crust. Sedimentary rocks are only a thin veneer over a crust consisting mainly of igneous and metamorphic rocks.

Sedimentary rocks are deposited in layers as strata, forming a structure called bedding. The study of sedimentary rocks and rock strata provides information about the subsurface that is useful for civil engineering, for example in the construction of roads, houses, tunnels, canals or other constructions. Sedimentary rocks are also important sources of natural resources like coal, fossil fuels, drinking water or ores.

The study of the sequence of sedimentary rock strata is the main source for scientific knowledge about the Earth's history, including palaeogeography, paleoclimatology and the history of life.

The scientific discipline that studies the properties and origin of sedimentary rocks is called sedimentology. Sedimentology is both part of geology and physical geography and overlaps partly with other disciplines in the Earth sciences, such as pedology, geomorphology, geochemistry or structural geology.

Based on the processes responsible for their formation, sedimentary rocks can be subdivided into four groups: clastic sedimentary rocks, biochemical (or biogenic) sedimentary rocks, chemical sedimentary rocks and a fourth category for 'other' sedimentary rocks formed by impacts, volcanism, and other minor processes.

Clastic Sedimentary Rocks

Clastic sedimentary rocks are composed of silicate minerals and rock fragments that were transported by moving fluids (as bed load, suspended load, or by sediment gravity flows) and were deposited when these fluids came to rest. Clastic rocks are composed largely of quartz, feldspar, rock (lithic) fragments, clay minerals, and mica; numerous other minerals may be present as accessories and may be important locally.

Clastic sediment, and thus clastic sedimentary rocks, are subdivided according to the dominant particle size (diameter). Most geologists use the Udden-Wentworth grain size scale and divide unconsolidated sediment into three fractions: gravel (>2 mm diameter), sand (1/16 to 2 mm diameter), and mud (clay is <1/256 mm and silt is between 1/16 and 1/256 mm). The classification of clastic sedimentary rocks parallels this scheme; conglomerates and breccias are made mostly of gravel, sandstones are made mostly of sand, and mudrocks are made mostly of mud. This tripartite subdivision is mirrored by the broad categories of rudites, arenites, and lutites, respectively, in older literature.

Subdivision of these three broad categories is based on differences in clast shape (conglomerates and breccias), composition (sandstones), grain size and/or texture (mudrocks).

Conglomerates and Breccias

Conglomerates are dominantly composed of rounded gravel and breccias are composed of dominantly angular gravel.

Sandstones

Sandstone classification schemes vary widely, but most geologists have adopted the Dott scheme, which uses the relative abundance of quartz, feldspar, and lithic framework grains and the abundance of muddy matrix between these larger grains.

Composition of Framework Grains

The relative abundance of sand-sized framework grains determines the first word in a sandstone name. For naming purposes, the abundance of framework grains is normalized to quartz, feldspar, and lithic fragments formed from other rocks. These are the three most abundant components of sandstones; all other minerals are considered accessories and not used in the naming of the rock, regardless of abundance.

- Quartz sandstones have >90 per cent quartz grains
- Feldspathic sandstones have <90 per cent quartz grains and more feldspar grains than lithic grains
- Lithic sandstones have <90 per cent quartz grains and more lithic grains than feldspar grains

Abundance of Muddy Matrix Between Sand Grains

When sand-sized particles are deposited, the space between the sand grains either remains open or is filled with mud (silt and/or clay sized particle).

- 'Clean' sandstones with open pore space (that may later be filled with cement) are called arenites;
- Muddy sandstones with abundant (>10%) muddy matrix are called wackes.

Six sandstone names are possible using descriptors for grain composition (quartz-, feldspathic-, and lithic-) and amount of matrix (wacke or arenite). For example, a quartz arenite would be composed of mostly (>90%) quartz grains and have little/no clayey matrix between the grains, a lithic wacke would have abundant lithic grains (<90% quartz, remainder would have more lithics than feldspar) and abundant muddy matrix, etc.

Although the Dott classification scheme is widely used by sedimentologists, common names like greywacke, arkose, and quartz sandstone are still widely used by nonspecialists and in popular literature.

Mudrocks

Mudrocks are sedimentary rocks composed of at least 50 per cent silt- and clay-sized particles. These relatively fine-grained particles are commonly transported as suspended particles by turbulent flow in water or air, and deposited as the flow calms and the particles settle out of suspension.

Most authors presently use the term 'mudrock' to refer to all rocks composed dominantly of mud. Mudrocks can be divided into siltstones (composed dominantly of silt-sized particles), mudstones (subequal mixture of silt- and clay-sized particles), and claystones (composed mostly of clay-sized particles). Most authors use 'shale' is a term for a fissile mudrock (regardless of grain size), although some older literature uses the term 'shale' as a synonym for mudrock.

Biochemical Sedimentary Rocks

Biochemical sedimentary rocks are created when organisms use materials dissolved in air or water to build their tissue. Examples include:

- Most types of limestone are formed from the calcareous skeletons of organisms such as corals, mollusks, and foraminifera.
- Coal which forms as plants remove carbon from the atmosphere and combine ith with other elements to build their tissue.
- Deposits of chert formed from the accumulation of siliceous skeletons from microscopic organisms such as radiolaria and diatoms.

Chemical Sedimentary Rocks

Chemical sedimentary rock forms when mineral constituents in solution become supersaturated and inorganically precipitate. Common chemical sedimentary rocks include oolitic limestone and rocks composed of evaporite minerals such as halite (rock salt), sylvite, barite and gypsum.

'Other' Sedimentary Rocks

This fourth miscellaneous category includes rocks formed by Pyroclastic flows, impact breccias, volcanic breccias, and other relatively uncommon processes.

Compositional Classification Schemes

Alternately, sedimentary rocks can be subdivided into compositional groups based on their mineralogy:

- ***Siliciclastic sedimentary rocks***, as described above, are dominantly composed of silicate minerals. The sediment that makes up these rocks was transported as bed load, suspended load, or by sediment gravity flows. Siliciclastic sedimentary rocks are subdivided into conglomerates and breccias, sandstone, and mudrocks.

- ***Carbonate sedimentary rocks*** are composed of calcite (rhombohedral $CaCO_3$), aragonite (orthorhombic $CaCO_3$), dolomite ($CaMg(CO_3)_2$), and other carbonate minerals based on the CO_3^{2-} ion. Common examples include limestone and dolostone.
- ***Evaporite sedimentary rocks*** are composed of minerals formed from the evaporation of water. The most common evaporite minerals are carbonates (calcite and others based on CO_3^{2-}), chlorides (halite and others built on Cl^-), and sulfates (gypsum and others built on SO_4^{2-}). Evaporite rocks commonly include abundant halite (rock salt), gypsum, and anhydrite.
- ***Organic-rich sedimentary rocks*** have significant amounts of organic material, generally in excess of 5 per cent total organic carbon. Common examples include coal, oil shale, and other sedimentary rocks that act as reservoirs for liquid hydrocarbons and natural gas.
- ***Siliceous sedimentary rocks*** are almost entirely composed of silica (SiO_2), typically as chert, opal, chalcedony or other microcrystalline forms.
- ***Iron-rich sedimentary rocks*** are composed of >15 per cent iron; the most common forms are banded iron formations and ironstones.
- ***Phosphatic sedimentary rocks*** are composed of phosphate minerals and contain more than 6.5 per cent phosphorus; examples include deposits of phosphate nodules, bone beds, and phosphatic mudrocks.

Formation

Sedimentary rocks are formed when sediment is deposited out of air, ice, wind, gravity, or water flows carrying the particles in suspension. This sediment is often formed when weathering and erosion break down a rock into loose material in a source area. The material is then transported from the source area to the deposition area. The type of sediment transported depends on the geology of the hinterland (the source area of the sediment). However, some sedimentary rocks, like evaporites, are composed of material that formed at the place of deposition. The nature of a sedimentary rock therefore not only depends on sediment supply, but also on the sedimentary depositional environment in which it formed.

Sedimentary Environments

The setting in which a sedimentary rock forms is called the sedimentary environment. Every environment has a characteristic combination of geologic processes and circumstances. The type of sediment that is deposited is not only dependent on the sediment that is transported to a place, but also on the environment itself.

A marine environment means the rock was formed in a sea or ocean. Often, a distinction is made between deep and shallow marine environments. Deep marine usually refers to environments more than 200 m below the water surface. Shallow marine environments exist adjacent to coastlines and can extend out to the boundaries of the continental shelf. The water in such environments has a generally higher energy than that in deep environments, because of wave activity. This means coarser sediment particles can be transported and the deposited sediment can be coarser than in deep environments. When the available sediment is transported from the continent, an alternation of sand, clay and silt is deposited. When the continent is far away, the amount of such sediment brought in may be small, and biochemical processes dominate the type of rock that forms. Especially in warm climates, shallow marine environments far offshore mainly see deposition of carbonate rocks. The shallow, warm water is an ideal habitat for many small organisms that build carbonate skeletons. When these organisms die their skeletons sink to the bottom, forming a thick layer of calcareous mud that may lithify into limestone. Warm shallow marine environments also are ideal environments for coral reefs, where the sediment consists mainly of the calcareous skeletons of larger organisms.

In deep marine environments, the water current over the sea bottom is small. Only fine particles can be transported to such places. Typically sediments depositing on the ocean floor are fine clay or small skeletons of micro-organisms. At 4 km depth, the solubility of carbonates increases dramatically (the depth zone where this happens is called the lysocline). Calcareous sediment that sinks below the lysocline dissolve, so no limestone can be formed below this depth. Skeletons of micro-organisms formed of silica (such as radiolarians) still deposit though. An example of a rock formed out of silica skeletons is radiolarite. When the bottom of the sea has a small inclination, for example at the continental slopes, the sedimentary cover can become unstable, causing turbidity currents. Turbidity currents are sudden disturbances of the normally quite deep marine environment and can cause the geologically speaking instantaneous deposition of large amounts of sediment, such as sand and silt. The rock sequence formed by a turbidity current is called a turbidite.

The coast is an environment dominated by wave action. At the beach, dominantly coarse sediment like sand or gravel is deposited, often mingled with shell fragments. Tidal flats and shoals are places that sometimes dry out because of the tide. They are often cross-cut by gullies, where the current is strong and the grain size of the deposited sediment is larger. Where along a coast (either the coast of a sea or a lake) rivers enter the body of water, deltas can form. These are large accumulations of sediment transported from the continent to places in front of the mouth of the river. Deltas are dominantly composed of clastic sediment.

A sedimentary rock formed on the land has a continental sedimentary environment. Examples of continental environments are lagoons, lakes, swamps, floodplains and alluvial fans. In the quiet water of swamps, lakes and lagoons, fine sediment is deposited, mingled with organic material from dead plants and animals. In rivers, the energy of the water is much higher and the transported material consists of clastic sediment. Besides transport by water, sediment can in continental environments also be transported by wind or glaciers. Sediment transported by wind is called aeolian and is always very well sorted, while sediment transported by a glacier is called glacial and is characterized by very poor sorting.

Sedimentary Facies

Sedimentary environments usually exist alongside each other in certain natural successions. A beach, where sand and gravel is deposited, is usually bounded by a deeper marine environment a little offshore, where finer sediments are deposited at the same time. Behind the beach, there can be dunes (where the dominant deposition is well sorted sand) or a lagoon (where fine clay and organic material is deposited). Every sedimentary environment has its own characteristic deposits. The typical rock formed in a certain environment is called its sedimentary facies. When sedimentary strata accumulate through time, the environment can shift, forming a change in facies in the subsurface at one location. On the other hand, when a rock layer with a certain age is followed laterally, the lithology (the type of rock) and facies eventually change.

Facies can be distinguished in a number of ways: the most common ways are by the lithology (for example: limestone, siltstone or sandstone) or by fossil content. Coral for example only lives in warm and shallow marine environments and fossils of coral are thus typical for shallow marine facies. Facies determined by lithology are called lithofacies; facies determined by fossils are biofacies.

Sedimentary environments can shift their geographical positions through time. Coastlines can shift in the direction of the sea when the sea level drops, when the surface rises due to tectonic forces in the Earth's crust or when a river forms a large delta. In the subsurface, such geographic shifts of sedimentary environments of the past are recorded in shifts in sedimentary facies. This means that sedimentary facies can change either parallel or perpendicular to an imaginary layer of rock with a fixed age, a phenomenon described by Walther's facies rule.

The situation in which coastlines move in the direction of the continent is called transgression. In the case of transgression, deeper marine facies are deposited over shallower facies, a succession called onlap. Regression is the situation in which a coastline moves in the direction of the sea. With regression, shallower facies are deposited on top of deeper facies, a situation called offlap.

The facies of all rocks of a certain age can be plotted on a map to give an overview of the palaeogeography. A sequence of maps for different ages can give an insight in the development of the regional geography.

Sedimentary Basins

Places where large-scale sedimentation takes place are called sedimentary basins. The amount of sediment that can be deposited in a basin depends on the depth of the basin, the so called accommodation space. Depth, shape and size of a basin depend on tectonics, movements within the Earth's lithosphere. Where the lithosphere moves upward (tectonic uplift), land eventually rises above sea level, so that and erosion removes material, and the area becomes a source for new sediment. Where the lithosphere moves downward (tectonic subsidence), a basin forms and sedimentation can take place. When the lithosphere keeps subsiding, new accommodation space keeps being created.

A type of basin formed by the moving apart of two pieces of a continent is called a rift basin. Rift basins are elongated, narrow and deep basins. Due to divergent movement, the lithosphere is stretched and thinned, so that the hot asthenosphere rises and heats the overlying rift basin. Apart from continental sediments, rift basins normally also have part of their infill consisting of volcanic deposits. When the basin grows due to continued stretching of the lithosphere, the rift grows and the sea can enter, forming marine deposits.

When a piece of lithosphere that was heated and stretched cools again, its density rises, causing isostatic subsidence. If this subsidence continues long enough the basin is called a sag basin. Examples of sag basins are the regions along passive continental margins, but sag basins can also be found in the interior of continents. In sag basins, the extra weight of the newly deposited sediments is enough to keep the subsidence going in a vicious circle. The total thickness of the sedimentary infill in a sag basins can thus exceed 10 km.

A third type of basin exists along convergent plate boundaries - places where one tectonic plate moves under another into the asthenosphere. The subducting plate bends and forms a fore-arc basin in front of the overriding plate– an elongated, deep asymmetric basin. Fore-arc basins are filled with deep marine deposits and thick sequences of turbidites. Such infill is called flysch. When the convergent movement of the two plates results in continental collision, the basin becomes shallower and develops into a foreland basin. At the same time, tectonic uplift forms a mountain belt in the overriding plate, from which large amounts of material are eroded and transported to the basin. Such erosional material of a growing mountain chain is called molasse and has either a shallow marine or a continental facies.

At the same time, the growing weight of the mountain belt can cause isostatic subsidence in the area of the overriding plate on the other side to the mountain belt. The basin type resulting from this subsidence is called a back-arc basin and is usually filled by shallow marine deposits and molasse.

Influence of Astronomical Cycles

In many cases facies changes and other lithological features in sequences of sedimentary rock have a cyclic nature. This cyclic nature was caused by cyclic changes in sediment supply and the sedimentary environment. Most of these cyclic changes are caused by astronomic cycles. Short astronomic cycles can be the difference between the tides or the spring tide every two weeks. On a larger time-scale, cyclic changes in climate and sea level are caused by Milankovitch cycles: cyclic changes in the orientation and/or position of the Earth's rotational axis and orbit around the Sun. There are a number of Milankovitch cycles known, lasting between 10,000 and 200,000 years.

Relatively small changes in the orientation of the Earth's axis or length of the seasons can be a major influence on the Earth's climate. An example are the ice ages of the past 2.6 million years (the Quaternary period), which are assumed to have been caused by astronomic cycles. Climate change can influence the global sea level (and thus the amount of accommodation space in sedimentary basins) and sediment supply from a certain region. Eventually, small changes in astronomic parameters can cause large changes in sedimentary environment and sedimentation.

Sedimentation Rates

The rate at which sediment is deposited differs depending on the location. A channel in a tidal flat can see the deposition of a few metres of sediment in one day, while on the deep ocean floor each year only a few millimetres of sediment accumulate. A distinction can be made between normal sedimentation and sedimentation caused by catastrophic processes. The latter category includes all kinds of sudden exceptional processes like mass movements, rock slides or flooding. Catastrophic processes can see the sudden deposition of a large amount of sediment at once. In some sedimentary environments, most of the total column of sedimentary rock was formed by catastrophic processes, even though the environment is usually a quiet place. Other sedimentary environments are dominated by normal, ongoing sedimentation.

In some sedimentary environments, sedimentation only occurs in some places. In a desert, for example, the wind deposits siliciclastic material (sand or silt) in some spots, or catastrophic flooding of a wadi may cause sudden deposis of large quantities of detrital material, but in most places eolian erosion dominates. The amount of sedimentary rock that forms is not only dependent on the amount of supplied material, but also on how well the material consolidates. Erosion removes most deposited sediment shortly after deposition.

Diagenesis

Pressure solution at work in a clastic rock. While material dissolves at places where grains are in contact, material crystallizes from the solution (as cement) in open pore spaces. This means there is a net flow of material from areas under high stress to those under low stress. As a result, the rock becomes more compact and harder. Loose sand can become sandstone in this way.

The term diagenesis is used to describe all the chemical, physical, and biological changes, including cementation, undergone by a sediment after its initial deposition, exclusive of surface weathering. Some of these processes cause the sediment to consolidate: a compact, solid substance forms out of loose material. Young sedimentary rocks, especially those of Quaternary age (the most recent period of the geologic time scale) are often still unconsolidated. As sediment deposition builds up, the overburden (or lithostatic) pressure rises and a process known as lithification takes place.

Sedimentary rocks are often saturated with seawater or groundwater, in which minerals can dissolve or from which minerals can precipitate. Precipitating minerals reduce the pore space in a rock, a process called cementation. Due to the decrease in pore space, the original connate fluids are expelled. The precipitated minerals form a cement and make the rock more compact and competent. In this way, loose clasts in a sedimentary rock can become 'glued' together.

When sedimentation continues, an older rock layer becomes buried deeper as a result. The lithostatic pressure in the rock increases due to the weight of the overlying sediment. This causes compaction, a process in which grains mechanical reorganize. Compaction is, for example, an important diagenetic process in clay, which can initially consist of 60 per cent water. During compaction, this interstitial water is pressed out of . paction can also be due to chemical processes, such as pressure solution. Pressure solution means material is going into solution at areas under high stress. The dissolved material precipitates again in open pore spaces, which menas there is a nett flow of material into the pores. However, in some cases a certain mineral dissolves and not precipitate again. This process is called leaching and increases pore space in the rock.

Some biochemical processes, like the activity of bacteria, can affect minerals in a rock and are therefore seen as part of diagenesis. Fungi and plants (by their roots) and various other organisms that live beneath the surface can also influence diagenesis.

Burial of rocks due to ongoing sedimentation leads to increased pressure and temperature, which stimulates certain chemical reactions. An example is the reactions by which organic material becomes lignite or coal. When temperature and pressure increase still further, the realm of diagenesis makes way for metamorphism, the process that forms metamorphic rock.

Colour

The colour of a sedimentary rock is often mostly determined by iron, an element with two major oxides: iron(II) oxide and iron(III) oxide. Iron(II) oxide only forms under anoxic circumstances and gives the rock a grey or greenish colour. Iron(III) oxide is often in the form of the mineral hematite and gives the rock a reddish to brownish colour. In arid continental climates rocks are in direct contact with the atmosphere, and oxidation is an important process, giving the rock a red or orange colour. Thick sequences of red sedimentary rocks formed in arid climates are called red beds. However, a red colour does not necessarily mean the rock formed in a continental environment or arid climate.

The presence of organic material can colour a rock black or grey. Organic material is in nature formed from dead organisms, mostly plants. Normally, such material eventually decays by oxidation or bacterial activity. Under anoxic circumstances, however, organic material cannot decay and becomes a dark sediment, rich in organic material. This, can for example, occur at the bottom of deep seas and lakes. There is little water current in such environments, so oxygen from surface water is not brought down, and the deposited sediment is normally a fine dark clay. Dark rocks rich in organic material are therefore often shales.

Texture

The size, form and orientation of clasts or minerals in a rock is called its texture. The texture is a small-scale property of a rock, but determined many of its large-scale properties, such as the density, porosity or permeabililty.

Clastic rocks have a 'clastic texture', which means they consist of clasts. The 3D orientation of these clasts is called the fabric of the rock. Between the clasts the rock can be composed of a matrix or a cement (the latter can consist of crystals of one or more precipitated minerals). The size and form of clasts can be used to determine the velocity and direction of current in the sedimentary environment where the rock was formed; fine, calcareous mud only settles in quiet water, while gravel and larger clasts are only deposited by rapidly moving water. The grain size of a rock is usually expressed with the Wentworth scale, though alternative scales are used sometimes. The grain size can be expressed as a diameter or a volume, and is always an average value — a rock is composed of clasts with different sizes. The statistical distribution of grain sizes is different for different rock types and is described in a property called the sorting of the rock. When all clasts are more or less of the same size, the rock is called 'well-sorted', when there is a large spread in grain size, the rock is called 'poorly sorted'.

Coquina, a rock composed of clasts of broken shells, can only form in energetic water. The form of a clast can be described by using four parameters:

1. *Surface texture* describes the amount of small-scale relief of the surface of a grain that is too small to influence the general shape.
2. *Rounding* describes the general smoothness of the shape of a grain.
3. Sphericity' describes the degree to which the grain approaches a sphere.
4. Grain form' describes the three dimensional shape of the grain.

Chemical sedimentary rocks have a non-clastic texture, consisting entirely of crystals. To describe such a texture only the average size of the crystals and the fabric are necessary.

Mineralogy

Most sedimentary rocks contain either quartz (especially siliciclastic rocks) or calcite (especially carbonate rocks). In contrast with igneous and metamorphic rocks, a sedimentary rocks usually contains very few different major minerals. However, the origin of the minerals in a sedimentary rock is often more complex than those in an igneous rock. Minerals in a sedimentary rock can have formed by precipitation during sedimentation or diagenesis. In the second case, the mineral precipitate can have grown over an older generation of cement. A complex diagenetic history can be studied by optical mineralogy, using a petrographic microscope.

Carbonate rocks dominantly consist of carbonate minerals like calcite, aragonite or dolomite. Both cement and clasts (including fossils and ooids) of a carbonate rock can consist of carbonate minerals. The mineralogy of a clastic rock is determined by the supplied material from the source area, the manner of transport to the place of deposition and the stability of a particular mineral. The stability of the major rock forming minerals (their resistance to weathering) is expressed by Bowen's reaction series. In this series, quartz is most stable, followed by feldspar, micas, and other less stable minerals that are only present when little weathering has occurred. The amount of weathering depends mainly on the distance to the source area, the local climate and the time it took for the sediment to be transported there. In most sedimentary rocks, mica, feldspar and less stable minerals have reacted to clay minerals like kaolinite, illite or smectite.

Primary Sedimentary Structures

Structures in sedimentary rocks can be divided in 'primary' structures (formed during deposition) and 'secondary' structures (formed after deposition). Unlike textures, structures are always large-scale features that can easily be studied in the field. Sedimentary structures can tell something about the sedimentary environment or can serve to tell which side originally faced up where tectonics have tilted or overturned sedimentary layers.

Sedimentary rocks are laid down in layers called beds or strata. A bed is defined as a layer of rock that has a uniform lithology and texture. Beds form by the deposition of layers of sediment on top of each other. The sequence of beds that characterizes sedimentary rocks is called bedding. Single beds can be a couple of centimetres to several meters thick. Finer, less pronounced layers are called laminae and the structure it forms in a rock is called lamination. Laminae are usually less than a few centimetres thick. Though bedding and lamination are often originally horizontal in nature, this is not always the case. In some environments, beds are deposited at a (usually small) angle. Sometimes multiple sets of layers with different orientations exist in the same rock, a structure called cross-bedding. Cross-bedding forms when small-scale erosion occurs during deposition, cutting off part of the beds. Newer beds then form at an angle to older ones.

The opposite of cross-bedding is parallel lamination, where all sedimentary layering is parallel. With laminations, differences are generally caused by cyclic changes in the sediment supply, caused for example by seasonal changes in rainfall, temperature or biochemical activity. Laminae that represent seasonal changes (like tree rings) are called varves. Some rocks have no lamination at all, their structural character is called massive bedding.

Graded bedding is a structure where beds with a smaller grain size occur on top of beds with larger grains. This structure forms when fast flowing water stops flowing. Larger, heavier clasts in suspension settle first, then smaller clasts. Though graded bedding can form in many different environments, it is characteristic for turbidity currents.

The bedform (the surface of a particular bed) can be indicative for a particular sedimentary environment too. Examples of bed forms are sole markings and ripple marks. Sole markings, such as tool marks and flute casts, are grove dug into a sedimentary layer that are preserved. These are often elongated structures and can be used to establish the direction of the flow during deposition.

Ripple marks also form in flowing water. There are two types: asymmetric wave ripples and symmetric current ripples. Environments where the current is in one direction, such as rivers, produce asymmetric ripples. The longer flank of such ripples is oriented opposite to the direction of the current. Wave ripples occur in environments where currents occur in all directions, such as tidal flats.

Another type of bed form are mud cracks, caused by the dehydration of sediment that occasionally comes above the water surface. Such structures are commonly found at tidal flats or point bars along rivers.

Sedimentary rocks are the only type of rock that can contain fossils, the remains or imprints of dead organisms. In nature, dead organisms are usually quickly removed by scavengers, bacteria, rotting and erosion. In some exceptional circumstances a carcass is fossilized because these natural processes are unable to work. The chance of fossilisation is higher when the sedimentation rate is high (so that a carcass is quickly buried), in anoxic environments (where little bacterial activity exists) or when the organism had a particularly hard skeleton. Larger, well-preserved fossils are relatively rare. Most sedimentary rocks contains fossils, though with many the fact only becomes apparent when studied under a microscope (microfossils) or with a loupe.

Fossils can both be the direct remains or imprints of organisms and their skeletons. Most commonly preserved are the harder parts of organisms such as bones, shells, woody tissue of plants. Soft tissue has a much smaller chance of being preserved and fossilized and soft tissue of animals older than 40 million years is very rare. Imprints of organisms made while still alive are called trace fossils. Examples are burrows, foot prints, etc.

Being part of a sedimentary rock, fossils undergo the same diagenetic processes as the rock. A shell consisting of calcite can for example dissolve, while a cement of silica then fills the cavity. In the same way, precipitating minerals can fill cavities formerly occupied by blood vessels, vascular tissue or other soft tissues. This preserves the form of the organism but changes the chemical composition, a process called permineralisation. The most common minerals in permineralisation cements are carbonates (especially calcite), forms of amorphous silica (chalcedony, flint, chert) and pyrite. In the case of silica cements, the process is called lithification.

At high pressure and temperature, the organic material of a dead organism undergoes chemical reactions in which volatiles like water and carbon dioxide are expulsed. The fossil, in the end, consists of a thin layer of pure carbon or its mineralized form, graphite. This form of fossilisation is called carbonisation. It is particularly important for plant fossils. The same process is responsible for the formation of fossil fuels like lignite or coal.

Secondary Sedimentary Structures

Secondary sedimentary structures are structures in sedimentary rocks which formed after deposition. Such structures form by chemical, physical and biological processes inside the sediment. They can be indicators for circumstances after deposition. Some can be used as way up criteria.

Organic presence in a sediment can leave more traces than just fossils. Preserved tracks and burrows are examples of trace fossils (also called ichnofossils). Some trace fossils such as paw prints of dinosaurs or early humans can capture human imagination, but such traces are relatively rare. Most trace fossils are burrows of molluscs or arthropods. This burrowing is called bioturbation by sedimentologists. It can be a valuable indicator of the biological and ecological environment after the sediment was deposited. On the other hand, the burrowing activity of organisms can destroy other (primary) structures in the sediment, making a reconstruction more difficult.

Secondary structures can also have been formed by diagenesis or the formation of a soil (pedogenesis) when a sediment is exposed above the water level. An example of a diagenetic structure common in carbonate rocks is a stylolite. Stylolites are iregular planes were material was dissolved into the pore fluids in the rock. The result of precipitation of a certain chemical species can be colouring and staining of the rock, or the formation of concretions. Concretions are roughly concentric bodies with a different composition from the host rock. Their formation can be the result of localized precipitation due to small differences in composition or porosity of the host rock, such as around fossils, inside burrows or around plant roots. In carbonate rocks such as limestone or chalk, chert or flint concretions are common, while terrestrial sandstones can have iron concretions. Calcite concretions in clay are called septarian concretions.

After deposition, physical processes can deform the sediment, forming a third class of secondary structures. Density contrasts between different sedimentary layers, such as between sand and clay, can result in flame structures or load casts, formed by inverted diapirism. The diapirism causes the denser upper layer to sink into the other layer. Sometimes, density contrast can result or grow when one of the lithologies dehydrates. Clay can be easily compressed as a result of dehydration, while sand retains the same volume and becomes relatively less dense. On the other hand, when the pore fluid pressure in a sand layer surpasses a critical point the sand can flow through overlying clay layers, forming discordant bodies of sedimentary rock called sedimentary dykes (the same process can form mud volcanoes on the surface).

A sedimentary dyke can also be formed in a cold climate where the soil is permanently frozen during a large part of the year. Frost weathering can form cracks in the soil that fill with rubble from above. Such structures can be used as climate indicators as well as way up structures.

Density contrasts can also cause small-scale faulting, even while sedimentation goes on (syn-sedimentary faulting). Such faulting can also occur when large masses of non-lithified sediment are deposited on a slope, such as at the front side of a delta or the continental slope. Instabilities in such sediments can result in slumping. The resulting structures in the rock are syn-sedimentary folds and faults, which can be difficult to distinguish from folds and faults formed by tectonic forces in lithified rocks.

That new rock layers are above older rock layers is stated in the principle of superposition. There are usually some gaps in the sequence called unconformities. These represent periods where no new sediments were laid down, or when earlier sedimentary layers raised above sea level and eroded away.

Sedimentary rocks contain important information about the history of the Earth. They contain fossils, the preserved remains of ancient plants and animals. Coal is considered a type of sedimentary rock. The composition of sediments provides us with clues as to the original rock. Differences between successive layers indicate changes to the environment over time. Sedimentary rocks can contain fossils because, unlike most igneous and metamorphic rocks, they form at temperatures and pressures that do not destroy fossil remains.

14 Weathering

Weathering is the breaking down of Earth's rocks, soils and minerals through direct contact with the planet's atmosphere. Weathering occurs *in situ*, or 'with no movement', and thus should not be confused with, which involves the movement of rocks and minerals by agents such as water, ice, wind, and gravity.

In addition, weathering is the effect of atmospheric exposure to man-made structures and materials.

Two important classifications of weathering processes exist – physical and chemical weathering. Mechanical or physical weathering involves the breakdown of rocks and soils through direct contact with atmospheric conditions, such as heat, water, ice and pressure. The second classification, chemical weathering, involves the direct effect of atmospheric chemicals or biologically produced chemicals (also known as biological weathering) in the breakdown of rocks, soils and minerals.

The materials left over after the rock breaks down combined with organic material creates soil. The mineral content of the soil is determined by the parent material, thus a soil derived from a single rock type can often be deficient in one or more minerals for good fertility, while a soil weathered from a mix of rock types (as in glacial, aeolian or alluvial sediments) often makes more fertile soil.

Physical Weathering

Physical weathering is the class of processes that causes the disintegration of rocks without chemical change. The primary process in physical weathering is abrasion (the process by which clasts and other particles are reduced in size). However, chemical and physical weathering often go hand in hand. For example, cracks exploited by physical weathering will increase the surface area exposed to chemical action. Furthermore, the chemical action at minerals in cracks can aid the disintegration process.

Thermal Stress

Thermal stress weathering (sometimes called insolation weathering) results from expansion or contraction of rock, caused by temperature changes. Thermal stress weathering comprises two main types, thermal shock and thermal fatigue. Thermal stress weathering is an important mechanism in deserts, where there is a large diurnal temperature range, hot in the day and cold at night. The repeated heating and cooling exerts stress on the outer layers of rocks, which can cause their outer layers to peel off in thin sheets. Although temperature changes are the principal driver, moisture can enhance thermal expansion in rock. Forest fires and range fires are also known to cause significant weathering of rocks and boulders exposed along the ground surface. Intense, localized heat can rapidly expand a boulder, causing its surface to exfoliate or spall.

Frost weathering or *cryofracturing* is the collective name for several processes where ice is present. This processes include frost shattering, frost-wedging and freeze-thaw weathering. This type of weathering is common in mountain areas where the temperature is around the freezing point of water. Certain frost-susceptible soils expand or heave upon freezing as a result of water migrating via capillary action to grow ice lenses near the freezing front. This same phenomena occurs within pore spaces of rocks. The ice accumulations grow larger as they attract liquid water from the surrounding pores. The ice crystal growth weakens the rocks which, in time, break up. It is caused by the expansion of ice when water freezes, so putting considerable stress on the walls of containment.

Freeze induced weathering action occurs mainly in environments where there is a lot of moisture, and temperatures frequently fluctuate above and below freezing point, especially in alpine and periglacial areas. An example of rocks susceptible to frost action is chalk, which has many pore spaces for the growth of ice crystals. This process can be seen in Dartmoor where it results in the formation of tors. When water that has entered the joints freezes, the ice formed strains the walls of the joints and causes the joints to deepen and widen. When the ice thaws, water can flow further into the rock. Repeated freeze-thaw cycles weaken the rocks which, over time, break up along the joints into angular pieces. The angular rock fragments gather at the foot of the slope to form a talus slope (or scree slope). The splitting of rocks along the joints into blocks is called block disintegration. The blocks of rocks that are detached are of various shapes depending on rock structure.

Pressure Release

In pressure release, also known as unloading, overlying materials (not necessarily rocks) are removed (by erosion, or other processes), which causes underlying rocks to expand and fracture parallel to the surface. Often the overlying material is heavy, and the underlying rocks experience high pressure under them, for example, a moving glacier. Pressure release may also cause exfoliation to occur.

Intrusive igneous rocks (e.g. granite) are formed deep beneath the Earth's surface. They are under tremendous pressure because of the overlying rock material. When erosion removes the overlying rock material, these intrusive rocks are exposed and the pressure on them is released. The outer parts of the rocks then tend to expand. The expansion sets up stresses which cause fractures parallel to the rock surface to form. Over time, sheets of rock break away from the exposed rocks along the fractures. Pressure release is also known as 'exfoliation' or 'sheeting'; these processes result in batholiths and granite domes, an example of which is Dartmoor.

Hydraulic Action

Hydraulic action occurs when water (generally from powerful waves) rushes rapidly into cracks in the rock face, thus trapping a layer of air at the bottom of the crack, compressing it and weakening the rock. When the wave retreats, the trapped air is suddenly released with explosive force. This explosive release of highly pressurized air blows fragments off of the rock face and thereby widens the crack.

Salt-crystal Growth

Salt crystallization, otherwise known as haloclasty, causes disintegration of rocks when saline (see salinity) solutions seep into cracks and joints in the rocks and evaporate, leaving salt crystals behind. These salt crystals expand as they are heated up, exerting pressure on the confining rock.

Salt crystallization may also take place when solutions decompose rocks (for example, limestone and chalk) to form salt solutions of sodium sulfate or sodium carbonate, of which the moisture evaporates to form their respective salt crystals.

The salts which have proved most effective in disintegrating rocks are sodium sulfate, magnesium sulfate, and calcium chloride. Some of these salts can expand up to three times or even more.

It is normally associated with arid climates where strong heating causes strong evaporation and therefore salt crystallization. It is also common along coasts. An example of salt weathering can be seen in the honeycombed stones in sea wall. Honeycomb is a type of tafoni, a class of cavernous rock weathering structures, which likely develop in large part by chemical and physical salt weathering processes.

Biological Weathering

Living organisms may contribute to mechanical weathering (as well as chemical weathering, see 'biological' weathering below). Lichens and mosses grow on essentially bare rock surfaces and create a more humid chemical microenvironment. The attachment of these organisms to the rock surface enhances physical as well as chemical breakdown of the surface microlayer of the rock. On a larger scale seedlings sprouting in a crevice and plant roots exert physical pressure as well as providing a pathway for water and chemical infiltration. Burrowing animals and insects disturb the soil layer adjacent to the bedrock surface thus further increasing water and acid infiltration and exposure to oxidation processes.

Chemical weathering changes the composition of rocks, often transforming them when water interacts with minerals to create various chemical reactions. Chemical weathering is a gradual and ongoing process as the mineralogy of the rock adjusts to the near surface environment. New or *secondary minerals* develop from the original minerals of the rock. In this the processes of oxidation and hydrolysis are most important.

Dissolution

Rainfall is acidic because atmospheric carbon dioxide dissolves in the rainwater producing weak carbonic acid. In unpolluted environments, the rainfall pH is around 5.6. Acid rain occurs when gases such as sulphur dioxide and nitrogen oxides are present in the atmosphere. These oxides react in the rain water to produce stronger acids and can lower the pH to 4.5 or even 3.0. Sulfur dioxide, SO_2, comes from volcanic eruptions or from fossil fuels, can become sulfuric acid within rainwater, which can cause solution weathering to the rocks on which it falls.

Some minerals, due to their natural solubility (e.g. evaporites), oxidation potential (iron-rich minerals, such as pyrite), or instability relative to surficial conditions will weather through dissolution naturally, even without acidic water.

One of the most well-known solution weathering processes is carbonation, the process in which atmospheric carbon dioxide leads to solution weathering. Carbonation occurs on rocks which contain calcium carbonate, such as limestone and chalk. This takes place when rain combines with carbon dioxide or an organic acid to form a weak carbonic acid which reacts with calcium carbonate (the limestone) and forms calcium bicarbonate. This process speeds up with a decrease in temperature, not because low temperatures generally drive reactions faster, but because colder water holds more dissolved carbon dioxide gas.

Carbonation is therefore a large feature of glacial weathering.

The reactions as follows:

- $CO_2 + H_2O => H_2CO_3$
- carbon dioxide + water => carbonic acid
- $H_2CO_3 + CaCO_3 => Ca(HCO_3)_2$
- carbonic acid + calcium carbonate => calcium bicarbonate

Carbonation on the surface of well-jointed limestone produces a dissected limestone pavement which is most effective along the joints, widening and deepening them.

Mineral hydration is a form of chemical weathering that involves the rigid attachment of H+ and OH- ions to the atoms and molecules of a mineral.

When rock minerals take up water, the increased volume creates physical stresses within the rock. For example iron oxides are converted to iron hydroxides and the hydration of anhydrite forms gypsum.

Hydrolysis on Silicates and Carbonates

Hydrolysis is a chemical weathering process affecting silicate and carbonate minerals. In such reactions, pure water ionizes slightly and reacts with silicate minerals. An example reaction:

$Mg_2SiO_4 + 4H^+ + 4OH^- = 2Mg^{2+} + 4OH^- + H_4SiO_4$

olivine (forsterite) + four ionized water molecules ? ions in solution + silicic acid in solution

This reaction results in complete dissolution of the original mineral, assuming enough water is available to drive the reaction. However, the above reaction is to a degree deceptive because pure water rarely acts as a H^+ donor. Carbon dioxide, though, dissolves readily in water forming a weak acid and H^+ donor.

$Mg_2SiO_4 + 4CO_2 + 4H_2O = 2Mg^{2+} + 4HCO_3^- + H_4SiO_4$

olivine (forsterite) + carbon dioxide + water ? Magnesium and bicarbonate ions in solution + silicic acid in solution

This hydrolysis reaction is much more common. Carbonic acid is consumed by silicate weathering, resulting in more alkaline solutions because of the bicarbonate. This is an important reaction in controlling the amount of CO_2 in the atmosphere and can affect climate.

Aluminosilicates when subjected to the hydrolysis reaction produce a secondary mineral rather than simply releasing cations.

$2KAlSi_3O_8 + 2H_2CO_3 + 9H_2O = Al_2Si_2O_5(OH)_4 + 4H_4SiO_4 + 2K^+ + 2HCO_3^-$

Orthoclase (aluminosilicate feldspar) + carbonic acid + water = Kaolinite (a clay mineral) + silicic acid in solution + potassium and bicarbonate ions in solution

Oxidation

Within the weathering environment chemical oxidation of a variety of metals occurs. The most commonly observed is the oxidation of Fe^{2+} (iron) and combination with oxygen and water to form Fe^{3+} hydroxides and oxides such as goethite, limonite, and hematite. This gives the affected rocks a reddish-brown coloration on the surface which crumbles easily and weakens the rock. This process is better known as 'rusting'. Many other metallic ores and minerals oxidize and hydrate to produce colored deposits, such as chalcopyrites or $CuFeS_2$ oxidizing to copper hydroxide and iron oxides.

Biological

A number of plants and animals may create chemical weathering through release of acidic compounds, i.e. moss on roofs is classed as weathering.

The most common form of biological weathering is the release of chelating compounds, i.e. acids, by plants so as to break down aluminium and iron containing compounds in the soils beneath them. Decaying remains of dead plants in soil may form organic acids which, when dissolved in water, cause chemical weathering. Extreme release of chelating compounds can easily affect surrounding rocks and soils, and may lead to podsolisation of soils.

Building Weathering

Buildings made of any stone, brick or concrete are susceptible to the same weathering agents as any exposed rock surface. Also statues, monuments and ornamental stonework can be badly damaged by natural weathering processes. This is accelerated in areas severely affected by acid rain.

15 Erosion

Erosion is the process of weathering and transport of solids (sediment, soil, rock and other particles) in the natural environment or their source and deposits them elsewhere. It usually occurs due to transport by wind, water, or ice; by down-slope creep of soil and other material under the force of gravity; or by living organisms, such as burrowing animals, in the case of bioerosion.

Erosion is a natural process, but it has been increased dramatically by human land use, especially industrial agriculture, deforestation, and urban sprawl. Land that is used for industrial agriculture generally experiences a significantly greater rate of erosion than that of land under natural vegetation, or land used for sustainable agricultural practices. This is particularly true if tillage is used, which reduces vegetation cover on the surface of the soil and disturbs both soil structure and plant roots that would otherwise hold the soil in place. However, improved land use practices can limit erosion, using techniques such as terrace-building, conservation tillage practices, and tree planting.

A certain amount of erosion is natural and, in fact, healthy for the ecosystem. For example, gravels continuously move downstream in watercourses. Excessive erosion, however, causes serious problems, such as receiving water sedimentation, ecosystem damage and outright loss of soil.

Erosion is distinguished from weathering, which is the process of chemical or physical breakdown of the minerals in the rocks, although the two processes may occur concurrently.

The rate of erosion depends on many factors. Climatic factors include the amount and intensity of precipitation, the average temperature, as well as the typical temperature range, and seasonality, the wind speed, storm frequency. The geologic factors include the sediment or rock type, its porosity and permeability, the slope (gradient) of the land, and whether the rocks are tilted, faulted, folded, or weathered. The biological factors include ground cover from vegetation or lack thereof, the type of organisms inhabiting the area, and the land use.

In general, given similar vegetation and ecosystems, areas with high-intensity precipitation, more frequent rainfall, more wind, or more storms are expected to have more erosion. Sediment with high sand or silt contents and areas with steep slopes erode more easily, as do areas with highly fractured or weathered rock. Porosity and permeability of the sediment or rock affect the speed with which the water can percolate into the ground. If the water moves underground, less runoff is generated, reducing the amount of surface erosion. Sediments containing more clay tend to erode less than those with sand or silt. Here, however, the impact of atmospheric sodium on erodibility of clay should be considered.

The factor that is most subject to change is the amount and type of ground cover. In an undisturbed forest, the mineral soil is protected by a litter layer and an organic layer. These two layers protect the soil by absorbing the impact of rain drops. These layers and the underlying soil in a forest are porous and highly permeable to rainfall. Typically, only the most severe rainfall and large hailstorm events will lead to overland flow in a forest. If the trees are removed by fire or logging, infiltration rates become high and erosion low to the degree the forest floor remains intact. Severe fires can lead to significantly increased erosion if followed by heavy rainfall. In the case of construction or road building, when the litter layer is removed or compacted, the susceptibility of the soil to erosion is greatly increased.

Roads are especially likely to cause increased rates of erosion because, in addition to removing ground cover, they can significantly change drainage patterns, especially if an embankment has been made to support the road. A road that has a lot of rock and one that is 'hydrologically invisible' (that gets the water off the road as quickly as possible, mimicking natural drainage patterns) has the best chance of not causing increased erosion.

Many human activities remove vegetation from an area, making the soil susceptible to erosion. Logging can cause increased erosion rates due to soil compaction, exposure of mineral soil, for example roads and landings. However it is the removal of or compromise to the forest floor not the removal of the canopy that can lead to erosion. This is because rain drops striking tree leaves coalesce with other rain drops creating larger drops. When these larger drops fall (called throughfall) they again may reach terminal velocity and strike the ground with more energy then had they fallen in the open. Terminal velocity of rain drops is reached in about 8 meters. Because forest canopies are usually higher than this, leaf drop can regain terminal velocity. However, the intact forest floor, with its layers of leaf litter and organic matter, absorbs the impact of the rainfall.

Heavy grazing can reduce vegetation enough to increase erosion. Changes in the kind of vegetation in an area can also affect erosion rates. Different kinds of vegetation lead to different infiltration rates of rain into the soil. Forested areas have higher infiltration rates, so precipitation will result in less surface runoff, which erodes. Instead much of the water will go in subsurface flows, which are generally less erosive. Leaf litter and low shrubs are an important part of the high infiltration rates of forested systems, the removal of which can increase erosion rates. Leaf litter also shelters the soil from the impact of falling raindrops, which is a significant agent of erosion. Vegetation can also change the speed of surface runoff flows, so grasses and shrubs can also be instrumental in this aspect.

One of the main causes of erosive soil loss in the year 2006 is the result of slash and burn treatment of tropical forest. When the total ground surface is stripped of vegetation and then seared of all living organisms, the upper soils are vulnerable to both wind and water erosion. In a number of regions of the earth, entire sectors of a country have been rendered unproductive. For example, on the Madagascar high central plateau, comprising approximately ten per cent of that country's land area, virtually the entire landscape is sterile of vegetation, with gully erosive furrows typically in excess of 50 metres deep and one kilometer wide. Shifting cultivation is a farming system which sometimes incorporates the slash and burn method in some regions of the world. This degrades the soil and causes the soil to become less and less fertile.

Approximately 40 per cent of the world's agricultural land is seriously degraded. According to the UN, an area of fertile soil the size of Ukraine is lost every year because of drought, deforestation and climate change. In Africa, if current trends of soil degradation continue, the continent might be able to feed just 25 per cent of its population by 2025, according to UNU's Ghana-based Institute for Natural Resources in Africa.

When land is overused by animal activities (including humans), there can be mechanical erosion and also removal of vegetation leading to erosion. In the case of the animal kingdom, this effect would become material primarily with very large animal herds stampeding such as the Blue Wildebeest on the Serengeti plain. Even in this case there are broader material benefits to the ecosystem, such as continuing the survival of grasslands, that are indigenous to this region. This effect may be viewed as anomalous or a problem only when there is a significant imbalance or overpopulation of one species.

In the case of human use, the effects are also generally linked to overpopulation. When large number of hikers use trails or extensive off road vehicle use occurs, erosive effects often follow, arising from vegetation removal and furrowing of foot traffic and off road vehicle tires. These effects can also accumulate from a variety of outdoor human activities, again simply arising from too many people using a finite land resource.

One of the most serious and long-running water erosion problems worldwide is in the People's Republic of China, on the middle reaches of the Yellow River and the upper reaches of the Yangtze River. From the Yellow River, over 1.6 billion tons of sediment flows into the ocean each year. The sediment originates primarily from water erosion in the Loess Plateau region of the northwest.

Gravity

Mass wasting is the down-slope movement of rock and sediments, mainly due to the force of gravity. Mass movement is an important part of the erosional process, as it moves material from higher elevations to lower elevations where other eroding agents such as streams and glaciers can then pick up the material and move it to even lower elevations. Mass-movement processes are always occurring continuously on all slopes; some mass-movement processes act very slowly; others occur very suddenly, often with disastrous results. Any perceptible down-slope movement of rock or sediment is often referred to in general terms as a landslide. However, landslides can be classified in a much more detailed way that reflects the mechanisms responsible for the movement and the velocity at which the movement occurs. One of the visible topographical manifestations of a very slow form of such activity is a scree slope.

Slumping happens on steep hillsides, occurring along distinct fracture zones, often within materials like clay that, once released, may move quite rapidly downhill. They will often show a spoon-shaped isostatic depression, in which the material has begun to slide downhill. In some cases, the slump is caused by water beneath the slope weakening it. In many cases it is simply the result of poor engineering along highways where it is a regular occurrence.

Surface creep is the slow movement of soil and rock debris by gravity which is usually not perceptible except through extended observation. However, the term can also describe the rolling of dislodged soil particles 0.5 to 1.0 mm in diametre by wind along the soil surface.

Splash erosion is the detachment and airborne movement of small soil particles caused by the impact of raindrops on soil.

Sheet erosion is the detachment of soil particles by raindrop impact and their removal downslope by water flowing overland as a sheet instead of in definite channels or rills. The impact of the raindrop breaks apart the soil aggregate. Particles of clay, silt and sand fill the soil pores and reduce infiltration. After the surface pores are filled with sand, silt or clay, overland surface flow of water begins due to the lowering of infiltration rates. Once the rate of falling rain is faster than infiltration, runoff takes place. There are two stages of sheet erosion. The first is rain splash, in which soil particles are knocked into the air by raindrop impact. In the second stage, the loose particles are moved downslope by broad sheets of rapidly flowing water filled with sediment known as sheetfloods. This stage of sheet erosion is generally produced by cloudbursts, sheetfloods commonly travel short distances and last only for a short time.

Rill erosion refers to the development of small, ephemeral concentrated flow paths, which function as both sediment source and sediment delivery systems for erosion on hillslopes. Generally, where water erosion rates on disturbed upland areas are greatest, rills are active. Flow depths in rills are typically on the order of a few centimetres or less and slopes may be quite steep. These conditions constitute a very different hydraulic environment than typically found in channels of streams and rivers. Eroding rills evolve morphologically in time and space. The rill bed surface changes as soil erodes, which in turn alters the hydraulics of the flow. The hydraulics is the driving mechanism for the erosion process, and therefore dynamically changing hydraulic patterns cause continually changing erosional patterns in the rill. Thus, the process of rill evolution involves a feedback loop between flow detachment, hydraulics, and bed form. Flow velocity, depth, width, hydraulic roughness, local bed slope, friction slope, and detachment rate are time and space variable functions of the rill evolutionary process. Superimposed on these interactive processes, the sediment load, or amount of sediment in the flow, has a large influence on soil detachment rates in rills. As sediment load increases, the ability of the flowing water to detach more sediment decreases.

Where precipitation rates exceed soil infiltration rates, *runoff* occurs. Surface runoff turbulence can often cause more erosion than the initial raindrop impact.

Gully erosion, also called *ephemeral gully erosion*, occurs when water flows in narrow channels during or immediately after heavy rains or melting snow. This is particularly noticeable in the formation of hollow ways, where, prior to being tarmacked, an old rural road has over many years become significantly lower than the surrounding fields.

A gully is sufficiently deep that it would not be routinely destroyed by tillage operations, whereas rill erosion is smoothed by ordinary farm tillage. The narrow channels, or gullies, may be of considerable depth, ranging from 1 to 2 feet (0.61 m) to as much as 75 to 100 feet (30 m). Gully erosion is not accounted for in the revised universal soil loss equation.

Valley or *stream erosion* occurs with continued water flow along a linear feature. The erosion is both downward, deepening the valley, and headward, extending the valley into the hillside. In the earliest stage of stream erosion, the erosive activity is dominantly vertical, the valleys have a typical V cross-section and the stream gradient is relatively steep. When some base level is reached, the erosive activity switches to lateral erosion, which widens the valley floor and creates a narrow floodplain. The stream gradient becomes nearly flat, and lateral deposition of sediments becomes important as the stream meanders across the valley floor. In all stages of stream erosion, by far the most erosion occurs during times of flood, when more and faster-moving water is available to carry a larger sediment load. In such processes, it is not the water alone that erodes: suspended abrasive particles, pebbles and boulders can also act erosively as they traverse a surface.

At extremely high flows, kolks, or vortices are formed by large volumes of rapidly rushing water. Kolks cause extreme local erosion, plucking bedrock and creating pothole-type geographical features called Rock-cut basins. Examples can be seen in the flood regions result from glacial Lake Missoula, which created the channeled scablands in the Columbia Basin region of eastern Washington.

Bank erosion is the wearing away of the banks of a stream or river. This is distinguished from changes on the bed of the watercourse, which is referred to as *scour*. Erosion and changes in the form of river banks may be measured by inserting metal rods into the bank and marking the position of the bank surface along the rods at different times.

Shoreline erosion, which occurs on both exposed and sheltered coasts, primarily occurs through the action of currents and waves but sea level (tidal) change can also play a role.

Hydraulic action takes place when air in a joint is suddenly compressed by a wave closing the entrance of the joint. This then cracks it. *Wave pounding* is when the sheer energy of the wave hitting the cliff or rock breaks pieces off. *Abrasion* or *corrasion* is caused by waves launching seaload at the cliff. It is the most effective and rapid form of shoreline erosion (not to be confused with *corrosion*). *Corrosion* is the dissolving of rock by carbonic acid in sea water. Limestone cliffs are particularly vulnerable to this kind of erosion. *Attrition* is where particles/seaload carried by the waves are worn down as they hit each other and the cliffs. This then makes the material easier to wash away. The material ends up as shingle and sand. Another significant source of erosion, particularly on carbonate coastlines, is the boring, scraping and grinding of organisms, a process termed *bioerosion*.

Sediment is transported along the coast in the direction of the prevailing current (longshore drift). When the upcurrent amount of sediment is less than the amount being carried away, erosion occurs. When the upcurrent amount of sediment is greater, sand or gravel banks will tend to form. These banks may slowly migrate along the coast in the direction of the longshore drift, alternately protecting and exposing parts of the coastline. Where there is a bend in the coastline, quite often a build up of eroded material occurs forming a long narrow bank (a spit). Armoured beaches and submerged offshore sandbanks may also protect parts of a coastline from erosion. Over the years, as the shoals gradually shift, the erosion may be redirected to attack different parts of the shore.

Ice erosion can take one of two forms. It can be caused by the movement of ice, typically as glaciers, in a process called *glacial erosion*. It can also be due to freeze-thaw processes in which water inside pores and fractures in rock may expand cause further cracking.

Glaciers erode predominantly by three different processes: abrasion/scouring, plucking, and ice thrusting. In an abrasion process, debris in the basal ice scrapes along the bed, polishing and gouging the underlying rocks, similar to sandpaper on wood. Glaciers can also cause pieces of bedrock to crack off in the process of plucking. In ice thrusting, the glacier freezes to its bed, then as it surges forward, it moves large sheets of frozen sediment at the base along with the glacier. This method produced some of the many thousands of lake basins that dot the edge of the Canadian Shield. These processes, combined with erosion and transport by the water network beneath the glacier, leave moraines, drumlins, ground moraine (till), kames, kame deltas, moulins, and glacial erratics in their wake, typically at the terminus or during glacier retreat.

Cold weather causes water trapped in tiny rock cracks to freeze and expand, breaking the rock into several pieces. This can lead to gravity erosion on steep slopes. The scree which forms at the bottom of a steep mountainside is mostly formed from pieces of rock (soil) broken away by this means. It is a common engineering problem wherever rock cliffs are alongside roads, because morning thaws can drop hazardous rock pieces onto the road.

In some places, water seeps into rocks during the daytime, then freezes at night. Ice expands, thus, creating a wedge in the rock. Over time, the repetition in the forming and melting of the ice causes fissures, which eventually breaks the rock down.

Wind

In arid climates, the main source of erosion is wind. The general wind circulation moves small particulates such as dust across wide oceans thousands of kilometers downwind of their point of origin, which is known as deflation. Erosion can be the result of material movement by the wind. There are two main effects. First, wind causes small particles to be lifted and therefore moved to another region. This is called deflation. Second, these suspended particles may impact on solid objects causing erosion by abrasion (ecological succession). Wind erosion generally occurs in areas with little or no vegetation, often in areas where there is insufficient rainfall to support vegetation. An example is the formation of sand dunes, on a beach or in a desert. Loess is a homogeneous, typically nonstratified, porous, friable, slightly coherent, often calcareous, fine-grained, silty, pale yellow or buff, windblown (aeolian) sediment. It generally occurs as a widespread blanket deposit that covers areas of hundreds of square kilometres and tens of metres thick. Loess often stands in either steep or vertical faces. Loess tends to develop into highly rich soils. Under appropriate climatic conditions, areas with loess are among the most agriculturally productive in the world. Loess deposits are geologically unstable by nature, and will erode very readily. Therefore, windbreaks (such as big trees and bushes) are often planted by farmers to reduce the wind erosion of loess.

Thermal

Thermal erosion is the result of melting and weakening permafrost due to moving water. It can occur both along rivers and at the coast. Rapid river channel migration observed in the Lena River of Siberia is due to thermal erosion, as these portions of the banks are composed of permafrost-cemented non-cohesive materials. Much of this erosion occurs as the weakened banks fail in large slumps. Thermal erosion also affects the Arctic coast, where wave action and near-shore temperatures combine to undercut permafrost bluffs along the shoreline and cause them to fail. Annual erosion rates along a 100-kilometre segment of the Beaufort Sea shoreline averaged 5.6 metres per year from 1955 to 2002.

Soil Erosion and Climate Change

The warmer atmospheric temperatures observed over the past decades are expected to lead to a more vigorous hydrological cycle, including more extreme rainfall events. In 1998 Karl and Knight reported that from 1910 to 1996 total precipitation over the contiguous U.S. increased, and that 53 per cent of the increase came from the upper 10 per cent of precipitation events (the most intense precipitation). The per cent of precipitation coming from days of precipitation in excess of 50 mm has also increased significantly.

Studies on soil erosion suggest that increased rainfall amounts and intensities will lead to greater rates of erosion. Thus, if rainfall amounts and intensities increase in many parts of the world as expected, erosion will also increase, unless amelioration measures are taken. Soil erosion rates are expected to change in response to changes in climate for a variety of reasons. The most direct is the change in the erosive power of rainfall. Other reasons include:

(a) changes in plant canopy caused by shifts in plant biomass production associated with moisture regime;

(b) changes in litter cover on the ground caused by changes in both plant residue decomposition rates driven by temperature and moisture dependent soil microbial activity as well as plant biomass production rates;

(c) changes in soil moisture due to shifting precipitation regimes and evapo-transpiration rates, which changes infiltration and runoff ratios;

(d) soil erodibility changes due to decrease in soil organic matter concentrations in soils that lead to a soil structure that is more susceptible to erosion and increased runoff due to increased soil surface sealing and crusting;

(e) a shift of winter precipitation from non-erosive snow to erosive rainfall due to increasing winter temperatures;

(f) melting of permafrost, which induces an erodible soil state from a previously non-erodible one; and

(g) shifts in land use made necessary to accommodate new climatic regimes.

Studies by Pruski and Nearing indicated that, other factors such as land use not considered, we can expect approximately a 1.7 per cent change in soil erosion for each 1 per cent change in total precipitation under climate change.

The removal by erosion of large amounts of rock from a particular region, and its deposition elsewhere, can result in a lightening of the load on the lower crust and mantle. This can cause tectonic or isostatic uplift in the region. Research undertaken since the early 1990s suggests that the spatial distribution of erosion at the surface of an orogen can exert a key influence on its growth and its final internal structure.

Materials Science

In materials science, erosion is the recession of surfaces by repeated localized mechanical trauma as, for example, by suspended abrasive particles within a moving fluid. Erosion can also occur from non-abrasive fluid mixtures. Cavitation is one example.

In hard particle erosion, the hardness of the impacted material is a large factor in the mechanics of the erosion. A soft material will typically erode fastest from glancing impacts. Harder material will typically erode fastest from perpendicular impacts. Hardness is a correlative factor for erosion resistance, but a higher hardness does not guarantee better resistance. Factors that affect the erosion rate also include impacting particle speed, size, density, hardness, and rotation. Coatings can be applied to retard erosion, but normally can only slow the removal of material. Erosion rate for solid particle impact is typically measured as mass of material removed divided by the mass of impacting material.

Figurative Use

The concept of erosion is commonly employed by analogy to various forms of perceived or real homogenization (i.e. erosion of boundaries), 'leveling out', collusion or even the decline of anything from morals to indigenous cultures. It is a common trope of the English language to describe as *erosion* the gradual, organic mutation of something thought of as distinct, more complex, harder to pronounce or more refined into something indistinct, less complex, easier to pronounce or (disparagingly) less refined.

16 Metamorphic Rock

Metamorphic rock is the transformation of an existing rock type, the *protolith*, in a process called metamorphism, which means 'change in form'. The protolith is subjected to heat and pressure (temperatures greater than 150 to 200° C and pressures of 1500 bars) causing profound physical and/or chemical change. The protolith may be sedimentary rock, igneous rock or another older metamorphic rock. Metamorphic rocks make up a large part of the Earth's crust and are classified by texture and by chemical and mineral assemblage (metamorphic facies). They may be formed simply by being deep beneath the Earth's surface, subjected to high temperatures and the great pressure of the rock layers above it. They can form from tectonic processes such as continental collisions, which cause horizontal pressure, friction and distortion. They are also formed when rock is heated up by the intrusion of hot molten rock called magma from the Earth's interior. The study of metamorphic rocks (now exposed at the Earth's surface following erosion and uplift) provides us with information about the temperatures and pressures that occur at great depths within the Earth's crust.

Some examples of metamorphic rocks are gneiss, slate, marble, schist, and quartzite.

Metamorphic minerals are those that form only at the high temperatures and pressures associated with the process of metamorphism. These minerals, known as index minerals, include sillimanite, kyanite, staurolite, andalusite, and some garnet.

Other minerals, such as olivines, pyroxenes, amphiboles, micas, feldspars, and quartz, may be found in metamorphic rocks, but are not necessarily the result of the process of metamorphism. These minerals formed during the crystallization of igneous rocks. They are stable at high temperatures and pressures and may remain chemically unchanged during the metamorphic process. However, all minerals are stable only within certain limits, and the presence of some minerals in metamorphic rocks indicates the approximate temperatures and pressures at which they formed.

The change in the particle size of the rock during the process of metamorphism is called recrystallization. For instance, the small calcite crystals in the sedimentary rock limestone change into larger crystals in the metamorphic rock marble, or in metamorphosed sandstone, recrystallization of the original quartz sand grains results in very compact quartzite, in which the often larger quartz crystals are interlocked. Both high temperatures and pressures contribute to recrystallization. High temperatures allow the atoms and ions in solid crystals to migrate, thus reorganizing the crystals, while high pressures cause solution of the crystals within the rock at their point of contact.

The layering within metamorphic rocks is called *foliation* (derived from the Latin word *folia*, meaning 'leaves'), and it occurs when a rock is being shortened along one axis during recrystallization. This causes the platy or elongated crystals of minerals, such as mica and chlorite, to become rotated such that their long axes are perpendicular to the orientation of shortening. This results in a banded, or foliated, rock, with the bands showing the colours of the minerals that formed them.

Textures are separated into foliated and non-foliated categories. Foliated rock is a product of differential stress that deforms the rock in one plane, sometimes creating a plane of cleavage. For example, slate is a foliated metamorphic rock, originating from shale. Non-foliated rock does not have planar patterns of strain.

Rocks that were subjected to uniform pressure from all sides, or those that lack minerals with distinctive growth habits, will not be foliated. Slate is an example of a very fine-grained, foliated metamorphic rock, while phyllite is medium, schist coarse, and gneiss very coarse-grained. Marble is generally not foliated, which allows its use as a material for sculpture and architecture.

Another important mechanism of metamorphism is that of chemical reactions that occur between minerals without them melting. In the process atoms are exchanged between the minerals, and thus new minerals are formed. Many complex high-temperature reactions may take place, and each mineral assemblage produced provides us with a clue as to the temperatures and pressures at the time of metamorphism.

Metasomatism is the drastic change in the bulk chemical composition of a rock that often occurs during the processes of metamorphism. It is due to the introduction of chemicals from other surrounding rocks. Water may transport these chemicals rapidly over great distances. Because of the role played by water, metamorphic rocks generally contain many elements absent from the original rock, and lack some that originally were present. Still, the introduction of new chemicals is not necessary for recrystallization to occur.

Contact Metamorphism

Contact metamorphism is the name given to the changes that take place when magma is injected into the surrounding solid rock (country rock). The changes that occur are greatest wherever the magma comes into contact with the rock because the temperatures are highest at this boundary and decrease with distance from it. Around the igneous rock that forms from the cooling magma is a metamorphosed zone called a *contact metamorphism aureole*. Aureoles may show all degrees of metamorphism from the contact area to unmetamorphosed (unchanged) country rock some distance away. The formation of important ore minerals may occur by the process of metasomatism at or near the contact zone.

When a rock is contact altered by an igneous intrusion it very frequently becomes more indurated, and more coarsely crystalline. Many altered rocks of this type were formerly called hornstones, and the term *hornfels* is often used by geologists to signify those fine grained, compact, non-foliated products of contact metamorphism. A shale may become a dark argillaceous hornfels, full of tiny plates of brownish biotite; a marl or impure limestone may change to a grey, yellow or greenish lime-silicate-hornfels or siliceous marble, tough and splintery, with abundant augite, garnet, wollastonite and other minerals in which calcite is an important component. A diabase or andesite may become a diabase hornfels or andesite hornfels with development of new hornblende and biotite and a partial recrystallization of the original feldspar. Chert or flint may become a finely crystalline quartz rock; sandstones lose their clastic structure and are converted into a mosaic of small close-fitting grains of quartz in a metamorphic rock called quartzite.

If the rock was originally banded or foliated (as, for example, a laminated sandstone or a foliated calc-schist) this character may not be obliterated, and a banded hornfels is the product; fossils even may have their shapes preserved, though entirely recrystallized, and in many contact-altered lavas the vesicles are still visible, though their contents have usually entered into new combinations to form minerals that were not originally present. The minute structures, however, disappear, often completely, if the thermal alteration is very profound; thus small grains of quartz in a shale are lost or blend with the surrounding particles of clay, and the fine ground-mass of lavas is entirely reconstructed.

By recrystallization in this manner peculiar rocks of very distinct types are often produced. Thus shales may pass into cordierite rocks, or may show large crystals of andalusite (and chiastolite), staurolite, garnet, kyanite and sillimanite, all derived from the aluminous content of the original shale. A considerable amount of mica (both muscovite and biotite) is often simultaneously formed, and the resulting product has a close resemblance to many kinds of schist. Limestones, if pure, are often turned into coarsely crystalline marbles; but if there was an admixture of clay or sand in the original rock such minerals as garnet, epidote, idocrase, wollastonite, will be present. Sandstones when greatly heated may change into coarse quartzites composed of large clear grains of quartz. These more intense stages of alteration are not so commonly seen in igneous rocks, because their minerals, being formed at high temperatures, are not so easily transformed or recrystallized.

In a few cases rocks are fused and in the dark glassy product minute crystals of spinel, sillimanite and cordierite may separate out. Shales are occasionally thus altered by basalt dikes, and feldspathic sandstones may be completely vitrified. Similar changes may be induced in shales by the burning of coal seams or even by an ordinary furnace.

There is also a tendency for metasomatism between the igneous magma and sedimentary country rock, whereby the chemicals in each are exchanged or introduced into the other. Granites may absorb fragments of shale or pieces of basalt. In that case, hybrid rocks called skarn arise, which don't have the characteristics of normal igneous or sedimentary rocks. Sometimes an invading granite magma permeates the rocks around, filling their joints and planes of bedding, etc., with threads of quartz and feldspar. This is very exceptional but instances of it are known and it may take place on a large scale.

Regional Metamorphism

Regional metamorphism is the name given to changes in great masses of rock over a wide area. Rocks can be metamorphosed simply by being at great depths below the Earth's surface, subjected to high temperatures and the great pressure caused by the immense weight of the rock layers above. Much of the lower continental crust is metamorphic, except for recent igneous intrusions. Horizontal tectonic movements such as the collision of continents create orogenic belts, and cause high temperatures, pressures and deformation in the rocks along these belts. If the metamorphosed rocks are later uplifted and exposed by erosion, they may occur in long belts or other large areas at the surface. The process of metamorphism may have destroyed the original features that could have revealed the rock's previous history. Recrystallization of the rock will destroy the textures and fossils present in sedimentary rocks. Metasomatism will change the original composition.

Regional metamorphism tends to make the rock more indurated and at the same time to give it a foliated, shistose or gneissic texture, consisting of a planar arrangement of the minerals, so that platy or prismatic minerals like mica and hornblende have their longest axes arranged parallel to one another. For that reason many of these rocks split readily in one direction along mica-bearing zones (schists). In gneisses, minerals also tend to be segregated into bands; thus there are seams of quartz and of mica in a mica schist, very thin, but consisting essentially of one mineral. Along the mineral layers composed of soft or fissile minerals the rocks will split most readily, and the freshly split specimens will appear to be faced or coated with this mineral; for example, a piece of mica schist looked at facewise might be supposed to consist entirely of shining scales of mica. On the edge of the specimens, however, the white folia of granular quartz will be visible. In gneisses these alternating folia are sometimes thicker and less regular than in schists, but most importantly less micaceous; they may be lenticular, dying out rapidly. Gneisses also, as a rule, contain more feldspar than schists do, and they are tougher and less fissile. Contortion or crumbling of the foliation is by no means uncommon, and then the splitting faces are undulose or puckered. Schistosity and gneissic banding (the two main types of foliation) are formed by directed pressure at elevated temperature, and to interstitial movement, or internal flow arranging the mineral particles while they are crystallizing in that directed pressure field. Rocks that were originally sedimentary and rocks that were undoubtedly igneous convert into schists and gneisses. If originally of similar composition they may be very difficult to distinguish from one another if the metamorphism has been great. A quartz-porphyry, for example, and a fine feldspathic sandstone, may both the converted into a grey or pink mica-schist. They are made by heat and pressure.

The five basic metamorphic textures with typical rock types are slaty (includes slate and phyllite) (the foliation is called 'slaty cleavage'), 'schistose' (includes schist) (the foliation is called ('schistosity'), gneissose (gneiss) (the foliation is called 'gneissosity'), granoblastic (includes granulite, some marbles and quartzite), and hornfelsic (includes hornfels and skarn).

Slate

Slate is a fine-grained, foliated, homogeneous metamorphic rock derived from an original shale-type sedimentary rock composed of clay or volcanic ash through low-grade regional metamorphism. The result is a foliated rock in which the foliation may not correspond to the original sedimentary layering. When expertly 'cut' by striking with a specialized tool in the quarry, many slates will form smooth flat sheets of stone which have long been used for roofing and floor tiles and other purposes. Slate is frequently grey in colour, especially when seen in masse covering roofs. However, slate occurs in a variety of colours even from a single locality; for example, slate from North Wales can be found in many shades of grey, from pale to dark, and may also be purple, green or cyan. Slate is not to be confused with shale, from which it may be formed, or schist. Ninety percent of Europe's natural slate used for roofing originates from Spain.

The word 'slate' is also used for some objects made from slate. It may mean a single roofing slate, or a writing slate, traditionally a small piece of slate, often framed in wood, used with chalk as a notepad or noticeboard etc, and especially for recording charges in pubs and inns. The phrase 'clean slate' or 'blank slate' comes from this use.

Before the mid-19th century, the terms *slate*, *shale* and *schist* were not sharply distinguished. In the context of underground coal mining, the term slate was commonly used to refer to shale well into the 20th century. For example, *roof slate* refers to shale above a coal seam, and *draw slate* refers to roof slate that falls from the mine roof as the coal is removed.

Mineral Composition

Slate is mainly composed of quartz and muscovite or illite, often along with biotite, chlorite, hematite, and pyrite and, less frequently, apatite, graphite, kaolin, magnetite, tourmaline, or zircon as well as feldspar. Occasionally, as in the purple slates of North Wales, ferrous reduction spheres form around iron nuclei, leaving a light green spotted texture. These spheres are sometimes deformed by a subsequent applied stress field to ovoids, which appear as ellipses when viewed on a cleavage plane of the specimen.

USES

Slate in Buildings

Slate can be made into roofing slates, also called *roofing shingles*, installed by a slater. Slate has two lines of breakability: cleavage and grain, which make it possible to split the stone into thin sheets. When broken, slate retains a natural appearance while remaining relatively flat and easily stackable.

Slate is particularly suitable as a roofing material as it has an extremely low water absorption index of less than 0.4 per cent. Its low tendency to absorb water also makes it very resistant to frost damage and breakage due to freezing.

Slate roof tiles are usually fixed using either nail fixing, or the hook fixing method as is common with Spanish slate. In the UK, nailing is typically done with double nails onto timber battens (England and Wales) or nailed directly onto timber sarking boards (Scotland and Northern Ireland). Nails will traditionally be copper, although modern alloy and stainless steel alternatives are known. Both these methods, if used properly, will provide a long-lasting weathertight roof with a typical lifespan of around 80-100 years.

Some mainland European slate suppliers suggest that using hook fixing means that :

- Areas of weakness on the tile are fewer since no holes have to be drilled.
- Roofing features such as valleys and domes are easier to create since narrow tiles can be used.
- Hook fixing is particularly suitable in regions subject to severe weather conditions since there is a greater resistance to wind uplift as the lower edge of the slate is secured.

The metal hooks are, however, visible and may be unsuitable for historic properties.

Slate tiles are often used for interior and exterior flooring, stairs, walkways and wall cladding. Tiles are installed and set on mortar and grouted along the edges. Chemical sealants are often used on tiles to improve durability and appearance, increase stain resistance, reduce efflorescence, and increase or reduce surface smoothness. Tiles are often sold gauged, meaning that the back surface is ground for ease of installation. Slate flooring can be slippery when used in external locations subject to rain.

Slate tiles were used in 19th century UK building construction (apart from roofs) and in slate quarrying areas such as Bethesda, Wales there are still many buildings wholly constructed of slate. Slates can also be set into walls to provide a rudimentary damp-proof membrane. Small offcuts are used as shims to level floor joists. In areas where slate is plentiful it is also used in pieces of various sizes for building walls and hedges, sometimes combined with other kinds of stone.

Because it is a good electrical insulator and fireproof, it was used to construct early-20th century electric switchboards and relay controls for large electric motors. Fine slate can also be used as a whetstone to hone knives.

Due to its thermal stability and chemical inertness, slate has been used for laboratory bench tops and for billiard table tops. In 18th- and 19th-century schools, slate was extensively used for blackboards and individual writing slates for which slate or chalk pencils were used.

In areas where it is available, high-quality slate is used for tombstones, commemorative tablets and by artists in various genres.

In Eurasia

Slate-producing regions in Europe include Wales , Cornwall (famously the village of Delabole), Cumbria in the

United Kingdom; parts of France (Anjou, Ardennes, Brittany, Savoie); Belgium (Ardenne); Liguria in northern Italy, especially between the town of Lavagna (which means chalkboard in Italian) and Fontanabuona valley; Portugal especially around Valongo in the north of the country; Germany's (Moselle River-region, Hunsrück, Eifel, Westerwald, Thuringia and north Bavaria); Alta, Norway (actually schist not a true slate) and Galicia. Some of the slate from Wales and Cumbria is coloured slate (non-blue): purple and formerly green in Wales and green in Cumbria. China has vast slate deposits; in recent years its export of finished and unfinished slate has increased, it has slate in various colours.

In the Americas

Slate is abundant in Brazil (the second-biggest producer of slate) around Papagaios in Minas Gerais (responsible for 95% of the extraction of slate in Brazil). An independent report by Consultant Geologist J. A. Walsh describes how certain products originating from Brazil on sale in the UK, are not entitled to bear the CE mark.

Other areas known for slate production are the east coast of Newfoundland, the Slate Belt of Eastern Pennsylvania, Buckingham County Virginia (Buckingham Slate), and the Slate Valley of Vermont and New York, where coloured slate is mined in the Granville, New York area.

A major slating operation existed in Monson, Maine, during the late 19th- and early-20th centuries. The slate found in Monson is usually a dark purple to blackish colour, and many local structures are still roofed with slate tiles. The roof of St. Patrick's Cathedral was made of roofing slate from Monson, as was the headstone of John F. Kennedy.

Slate is also found in the Arctic and was used by the Inuit to make the blades for ulus.

17 Limestone

Limestone is a sedimentary rock composed largely of the minerals calcite and/or aragonite, which are different crystal forms of calcium carbonate ($CaCO_3$).

Like most other sedimentary rocks, limestones are composed of grains; however, most grains in limestone are skeletal fragments of marine organisms such as coral or foraminifera. Other carbonate grains comprising limestones are ooids, peloids, intraclasts, and extraclasts. Some limestones do not consist of grains at all and are formed completely by the chemical precipitation of calcite or aragonite. i.e. travertine.

The solubility of limestone in water and weak acid solutions leads to karst landscapes. Regions overlying limestone bedrock tend to have fewer visible groundwater sources (ponds and streams), as surface water easily drains downward through joints in the limestone. While draining, water and organic acid from the soil slowly (over thousands or millions of years) enlarges these cracks; dissolving the calcium-carbonate and carrying it away in solution. Most cave systems are through limestone bedrock.

Limestone often contains variable amounts of silica in the form of chert (aka chalcedony, flint, jasper, etc.) or siliceous skeletal fragment (sponge spicules, diatoms, radiolarians), as well as varying amounts of clay, silt and sand sized terrestrial detritus carried in by rivers. The primary source of the calcite in limestone is most commonly marine organisms. These organisms secrete shells made of aragonite or calcite and leave these shells behind after the organism dies. Some of these organisms can construct mounds of rock known as reefs, building upon past generations. Below about 3,000 metres, water pressure and temperature causes the dissolution of calcite to increase non-linearly so that limestone typically does not form in deeper waters. Secondary calcite may also be deposited by supersaturated meteoric waters (groundwater that precipitates the material in caves). This produces speleothems such as stalagmites and stalactites. Another form taken by calcite is that of oolites (oolitic limestone) which can be recognized by its granular appearance.

Limestone makes up about 10 per cent of the total volume of all sedimentary rocks. Limestones may also form in both lacustrine and evaporite depositional environments.

Calcite can be either dissolved by groundwater or precipitated by groundwater, depending on several factors including the water temperature, pH, and dissolved ion concentrations. Calcite exhibits an unusual characteristic called retrograde solubility in which it becomes less soluble in water as the temperature increases.

When conditions are right for precipitation, calcite forms mineral coatings that cement the existing rock grains together or it can fill fractures.

Karst topography and caves develop in carbonate rocks due to their solubility in dilute acidic groundwater. Cooling groundwater or mixing of different groundwaters will also create conditions suitable for cave formation.

Coastal limestones are often eroded by organisms which bore into the rock by various means. Thi< process is known as bioerosion. It is most common in the tropics, and it is known throughout the fossil record.

Because of impurities, such as clay, sand, organic remains, iron oxide and other materials, many limestones exhibit different colours, especially on weathered surfaces. Limestone may be crystalline, clastic, granular, or massive, depending on the method of formation. Crystals of calcite, quartz, dolomite or barite may line small cavities in the rock. Folk and Dunham classifications are used to describe limestones more precisely.

Travertine is a banded, compact variety of limestone formed along streams, particularly where there are waterfalls and around hot or cold springs. Calcium carbonate is deposited where evaporation of the water leaves a solution that is supersaturated with chemical constituents of calcite. Tufa, a porous or cellular variety of travertine, is found near waterfalls. Coquina is a poorly consolidated limestone composed of pieces of coral or shells.

During regional metamorphism that occurs during the mountain building process (orogeny) limestone recrystallizes into marble.

Limestone is a parent material of Mollisol soil group.

Limestone is partially soluble, especially in acid, and therefore forms many erosional landforms. These include limestone pavements, pot holes, cenotes, caves and gorges. Such erosion landscapes are known as karsts. Limestone is less resistant than most igneous rocks, but more resistant than most other sedimentary rocks. Limestone is therefore usually associated with hills and downland and occurs in regions with other sedimentary rocks, typically clays.

Bands of limestone emerge from the Earth's surface in often spectacular rocky outcrops and islands. Examples include the Burren in Co. Clare, Ireland; the Verdon Gorge in France; Malham Cove in North Yorkshire and the Isle of

Wight, England; on Fårö near the Swedish island of Gotland, the Niagara Escarpment in Canada/United States, Notch Peak in Utah, the Ha Long Bay National Park in Vietnam and the hills around the Lijiang River and Guilin city in China.

The Florida Keys, islands off the south coast of Florida, are composed mainly of oolitic limestone (the Lower Keys) and the carbonate skeletons of coral reefs (the Upper Keys), which thrived in the area during interglacial periods when sea level was higher than at present.

Unique habitats are found on alvars, extremely level expanses of limestone with thin soil mantles. The largest such expanse in Europe is the Stora Alvaret on the island of Öland, Sweden. Another area with large quantities of limestone is the island of Gotland, Sweden. Huge quarries in northwestern Europe, such as those of Mount Saint Peter (Belgium/Netherlands), extend for more than a hundred kilometres.

The world's largest limestone quarry is at Michigan Limestone and Chemical Company in Rogers City, Michigan.

Uses

Limestone is very common in architecture, especially in Europe and North America. Many landmarks across the world, including the Great Pyramid and its associated Complex in Giza, Egypt, are made of limestone. So many buildings in Kingston, Canada were constructed from it that it is nicknamed the 'Limestone City'. On the island of Malta, a variety of limestone called Globigerina limestone was for a long time the only building material available, and is still very frequently used on all types of buildings and sculptures. Limestone is readily available and relatively easy to cut into blocks or more elaborate carving. It is also long-lasting and stands up well to exposure. However, it is a very heavy material, making it impractical for tall buildings, and relatively expensive as a building material.

Limestone was most popular in the late 19th and early 20th centuries. Train stations, banks and other structures from that era are normally made of limestone. Limestone is used as a facade on some skyscrapers, but only in thin plates for covering rather than solid blocks. In the United States, Indiana, most notably the Bloomington area, has long been a source of high quality quarried limestone, called Indiana limestone. Many famous buildings in London are built from Portland limestone.

Limestone was also a very popular building block in the Middle Ages in the areas where it occurred since it is hard, is durable, and commonly occurs in easily accessible surface exposures. Many mediaeval churches and castles in Europe are made of limestone. Beer stone was a popular kind of limestone for medieval buildings in southern England.

Limestone and (to a lesser extent) marble are reactive to acid solutions, making acid rain a significant problem to the preservation of artifacts made from this stone. Many limestone statues and building surfaces have suffered severe damage due to acid rain. Acid-based cleaning chemicals can also etch limestone, which should only be cleaned with a neutral or mild alkaline-based cleaner.

Other uses include:

- The manufacture of quicklime (calcium oxide) and slaked lime (calcium hydroxide);
- Cement and mortar;
- Pulverized limestone is used as a soil conditioner to neutralize acidic soil conditions;
- Crushed for use as aggregate—the solid base for many roads;
- Geological formations of limestone are among the best petroleum reservoirs;

- As a reagent in flue gas desulfurization (sulfur dioxide air pollution control);
- Glass making, in some circumstances;
- Added to paper, plastics, paint, tiles, and other materials as both white pigment and a cheap filler;
- Toothpaste;
- Suppression of methane explosions in underground coal mines;
- Added to bread and cereals as a source of calcium;
- Calcium supplement for poultry (when ground up);
- Remineralizing and increasing the alkalinity of purified water to prevent pipe corrosion and to return essential nutrients;
- Used in blast furnaces to extract iron from its ore;
- Medicines;
- Cosmetics;
- Art (sculptures).

18 Rock Types

Igneous

A sample of andesite (dark groundmass) with amygdaloidal vesicules filled with zeolite. Diametre of view is 8 cm.

Andesite — an Intermediate volcanic rock

Icelandite

Anorthosite — an igneous ultramafic rock composed predominantly of plagioclase

Aplite — a very fine grained intrusive igneous rock

Basalt — a volcanic rock of mafic composition

Adakite — a class of basaltic rocks containing relatively small amounts of the trace elements yttrium and ytterbium

Hawaiite — a class of basalts formed from Ocean Island (hot spot) magmatism

Picrite

Basanite — a volcanic rock of mafic composition; essentially a silica undersaturated basalt

Boninite — a high-magnesian basalt dominated by pyroxene

Carbonatite — a rare igneous rock composed of >50 per cent carbonate minerals

Charnockite — a rare type of granite containing pyroxene

Enderbite — a variety of charnockite

Dacite — a felsic to intermediate volcanic rock with high iron content

Diabase or dolerite — an intrusive mafic rock forming dykes or sills.

Diorite — a coarse grained intermediate plutonic rock composed of plagioclase, pyroxene and/or amphibole

Dunite — an ultramafic cumulate rock composed of olivine and accessories

Essexite — a silica undersaturated mafic plutonic rock (essentially a foid-bearing gabbro)

Foidolite — a plutonic igneous rock composed of >90 per cent feldspathoid minerals

Gabbro — a coarse grained plutonic rock composed of pyroxene and plagioclase basically equivalent to basalt

Granite — a coarse grained plutonic rock composed of orthoclase, plagioclase and quartz

Granodiorite — a granitic plutonic rock with plagioclase > orthoclase

Granophyre — a subvolcanic intrusive rock of granitic composition

Harzburgite — a variety of peridotite; an ultramafic cumulate rock

Hornblendite — a mafic or ultramafic cumulate rock dominated by >90 per cent hornblende

Hyaloclastite — a volcanic rock composed primarily of glasses and glassy tuff

Icelandite — a volcanic rock

Ignimbrite — a fragmental volcanic rock

Ijolite — a very rare silica-undersaturated plutonic rock

Limey shale overlaid by limestone. Cumberland Plateau, Tennessee

Kimberlite — a rare ultramafic, ultrapotassic volcanic rock and a source of diamonds

Komatiite — an ancient ultramafic volcanic rock

Lamproite — an ultrapotassic volcanic rock

Lamprophyre — an ultramafic, ultrapotassic intrusive rock dominated by mafic phenocrysts in a feldspar groundmass

Latite — a silica undersaturated form of andesite

Lherzolite — an ultramafic rock, essentially a peridotite

Monzogranite — a silica undersaturated granite with <5 per cent normative quartz

Monzonite — a plutonic rock with <5 per cent normative quartz

Nepheline syenite — a silica undersaturated plutonic rock with nepheline replacing orthoclase

Nephelinite — a silica undersaturated plutonic rock with >90 per cent nepheline

Norite — a hypersthene bearing gabbro

Obsidian — a type of volcanic glass

Pegmatite — an igneous rock (or metamorphic rock) with giant sized crystals

Peridotite — a plutonic or cumulate ultramafic rock composed of >90 per cent olivine

Phonolite — a silica undersaturated volcanic rock; essentially similar to nepheline syenite

Picrite — an olivine-bearing basalt

Porphyry — a rock, usually granitic, with a porphyritic texture

Pseudotachylite — a glass formed by melting within a fault via friction

Pumice — a fine grained, extremely vesicular volcanic rock

Pyroxenite — a coarse grained plutonic rock composed of >90 per cent pyroxene

Quartz diorite — a diorite with >5 per cent modal quartz

Quartz monzonite — an intermediate plutonic rock, essentially a monzonite with 5-10 per cent modal quartz

Rhyodacite — a felsic volcanic rock which is intermediate between a rhyolite and a dacite

Rhyolite — a felsic volcanic rock

Comendite — a peralkaline rhyolite

Pantellerite — an alkaline rhyolite-rhyodacite with amphibole phenocrysts

Scoria — an extremely vesicular mafic volcanic rock

Sovite — a coarse grained carbonatite rock

Syenite — a plutonic rock dominated by orthoclase feldspar; a type of granitoid

Tachylyte — essentially a basaltic glass

Tephrite — a silica undersaturated volcanic rock; can be a generic term

Tonalite — a plagioclase-dominant granitoid

Trachyandesite — an alkaline intermediate volcanic rock

Benmoreite — sodic trachyandesite

Basaltic trachyandesite

Mugearite — sodic basaltic trachyandesite

Shoshonite — potassic basaltic trachyandesite

Trachyte — a silica undersaturated volcanic rock; essentially a feldspathoid-bearing rhyolite

Troctolite — a plutonic ultramafic rock containing olivine, pyroxene and plagioclase

Trondhjemite — a form of tonalite where plagioclase-group feldspar is oligoclase

Tuff — a fine grained volcanic rock formed from volcanic ash

Websterite — a type of pyroxenite, composed of clinoproxene and orthopyroxene

Wehrlite — an ultramafic plutonic or cumulate rock, a type of peridotite, composed of olivine and clinopyroxene

Metamorphic

Anthracite — a type of coal

Amphibolite — a metamorphic rock composed primarily of amphibole

Epidiorite

Blueschist — a metamorphic rock composed of sodic amphiboles with a distinct blue colour

Banded gneiss with a dike of granite orthogneiss

Eclogite — an ultra-high grade metamorphosed basalt or gabbro; also a facies of metamorphic rocks

Gneiss — a coarse grained metamorphic rock

Gossan — the product of the weathering of a sulfide rock or ore body

Granulite — a high grade metamorphic rock formed from basalt; also a facies of metamorphic rocks

Greenschist — a generic term for a mafic metamorphic rock dominated by green amphiboles

Greenstone

Hornfels — a metamorphic rock formed by heating by an igneous rock

Marble

Marble — a metamorphosed limestone

Migmatite — a high grade metamorphic rock verging upon melting into a magma

Mylonite — a metamorphic rock formed by shearing

Pelite — a metamorphic rock with a protolith of clay-rich (siltstone) sedimentary rock

Phyllite — a low grade metamorphic rock composed mostly of micaceous minerals

Psammite — a metamorphic rock with a protolith of quartz-rich (sandstone) sedimentary rock

Quartzite — a metamorphosed sandstone typically composed of >95 per cent quartz

Manhattan Schist, from Southeastern New York

Schist — a low to medium grade metamorphic rock

Serpentinite — a metamorphosed ultramafic rock dominated by serpentine minerals

Skarn — a metasomatic rock

Slate — a low grade metamorphic rock formed from shale or silts

Suevite — a rock formed by partial melting during a meteorite impact

Talc carbonate — a metamorphosed ultramafic rock with talc as an essential constituent; similar to a serpentinite

Soapstone — essentially a talc schist

Specific Varieties of Rocks

The following terms are used to describe rocks which are not petrographically or genetically distinct, but are defined according to various other criteria; most are specific classes of other rocks, or altered versions of existing rocks. Some archaic and vernacular terms for rocks are also included.

Adamellite — a variety of quartz monzonite

Appinite — a group of varieties of lamprophyre, mostly rich in hornblende

Aphanite — an aphanitic felsic volcanic rock which confounds identification via optical means

Borolanite — a variety of nepheline syenite from Loch Borralan, Scotland

Blue Granite — essentially larvikite, a monzonite

Epidosite — a type of metasomatite; essentially altered basalt

Felsite — an aphanitic felsic volcanic rock which confounds identification via optical means

Flint — typically a form of chert, jasper, or tuff

Ganister — a Cornish term for a palaeosol formed on sandstone

Ijolite — a silica-undersaturated plutonic rock associated with nepheline syenites

Jadeitite — a very rare rock formed by concentration of jadeite pyroxene; a form of serpentinite

Jasperoid — a hematite-silica metasomatite analogous to a skarn

Kenyte — a variety of phonolite, first found on Mount Kenya

Vogesite — a variety of lamprophyre

Larvikite — a variety of monzonite with microperthitic ternary feldspars from Larvik, Norway

Litchfieldite — a metamorphosed nepheline syenite occurrence near Litchfield, Maine

Luxullianite — a tourmaline-bearing granite with a peculiar texture, occurring at Luxulyan, Cornwall, England

Mangerite — a hypersthene-bearing monzonite

Minette — a variety of lamprophyre

Novaculite — a chert formation found in Oklahoma, Arkansas and Texas

Pyrolite — a chemical analogue considered to theoretically represent the earth's upper mantle

Rapakivi granite — a granite which exhibits the peculiar rapakivi texture

Rhomb porphyry — a type of latite with euhedral rhombic phenocrysts of feldspar

Shonkinite — an archaic and informal term used to describe melitilic and kalsititic rocks; often used today

Taconite — a term for banded iron formation primarily used in the United States of America

Teschenite — essentially a silica undersaturated, analcime bearing gabbro

Theralite — essentially a nepheline gabbro

Variolite — devitrified glass

Rocks and Their Uses

Rocks normally consist of several minerals, some essential, some accessory. A rock may be thought of as a 'mineral environment'. Each rock type was formed under certain specific conditions, resulting in the formation of a fairly predictable group of minerals. Rocks fall into three classes according to their origin: Igneous-Sedimentary-Metamorphic.

COAL: A sedimentary rock, formed from decayed plants, is mainly used in power plants to make electricity.

LIMESTONE: A sedimentary rock, it is used mainly in the manufacture of Portland cement, the production of lime, manufacture of paper, petrochemicals, insecticides, linoleum, fiberglass, glass, carpet backing and as the coating on many types of chewing gum.

SHALE: A sedimentary rock, well stratified in thin beds. It splits unevenly more or less parallel to bedding plane and may contain fossils. It can be a component of bricks and cement.

CONGLOMERATE: A sedimentary rock with a variable hardness, consisted of rounded or angular rock or mineral fragments cemented by silica, lime, iron oxide, etc. Usually found in mostly thick, crudely stratified layers. Used in the construction industry.

SANDSTONE: A sedimentary rock more or less rounded. Generally thick-bedded, varicolored, rough feel due to uneven surface produced by breaking around the grains. Used principally for construction, it is easy to work, the red-brown sandstone of Triassic age, better known as 'brownstone', has been used in many eastern cities.

GRANITE: An igneous-plutonic rock, medium to coarse-grained that is high in silica, potassium, sodium and quartz but low in calcium, iron and magnesium. It is widely used for architectural construction, ornamental stone and monuments.

PUMICE: An igneous-volcanic rock, it is a porous, brittle variety of rhyolite and is light enough to float. It is formed when magma of granite composition erupts at the earth's surface or intrudes the crust at shallow depths. It is used as an abrasive material in hand soaps, emery boards, etc.

GABBRO: An igneous-plutonic rock, generally massive, but may exhibit a layered structure produced by successive layers of different mineral composition. It is widely used as crushed stone for concrete aggregate, road metal, railroad ballast, etc. Smaller quantities are cut and polished for dimension stone (called black granite).

BASALT: An igneous volcanic rock, dark gray to black, it is the volcanic equivalent of plutonic gabbro and is rich in ferromagnesian minerals. Basalt can be used in aggregate.

SCHIST: A metamorphic uneven-granular, medium to coarse grained, crystalline with prominent parallel mineral orientation. Goes from silvery white to all shades of gray with yellow to brown tones depending on the mineral concentration. Some schists have graphite and some are used as building stones.

GNEISS: A metamorphic uneven granular medium to coarse grained crystalline with more or less parallel mineral orientation. Colors are too variable to be of diagnostic value. Due to physical and chemical similarity between many gneisses and plutonic igneous rocks some are used as building stones and other structural purposes.

QUARTZITE: A metamorphic or sedimentary rock with crystalline texture, consists of rounded quartz grains cemented by crystalline quartz, generally white, light gray or yellow to brown. Same uses as sandstone.

MARBLE: A metamorphic even-granular grain to medium grained and may be uneven granular and coarse grained in calc-silicate rock. The normal colour is white but accessory minerals act as colouring agents and may produce a variety of colours. Depending upon its purity, texture, colour and marbled pattern it is quarried for use as dimension stone for statuary, architectural and ornamental purposes. Dolomite rich marble may be a source for magnesium and is used as an ingredient in the manufacture of refracting materials.

Index

H

I

L

S

❑❑❑